Super Steam
LOCOMOTIVES

1661

166
S

Brian Solomon

MBI Publishing Company

D E D I C A T I O N

In memory of my Grandfathers,
Alfred P. Solomon and Russell J. Daniel.
They would have greatly enjoyed this book.

First published in 2000 by MBI Publishing Company, 729 Prospect Avenue, PO Box 1, Osceola, WI 54020-0001 USA

MBI Publishing Company books are also available at discounts in bulk quantity for industrial or sales-promotional use. For details write to Special Sales Manager at Motorbooks International Wholesalers & Distributors, 729 Prospect Avenue, PO Box 1, Osceola, WI 54020-0001 USA.

Edited by Amy Glaser
Designed by Jim Snyder
Printed in China

Library of Congress Cataloging-in-Publication Data
Solomon, Brian.
    Super steam locomotives / Brian Solomon.
      p. cm.— (Enthusiast color series)
    ISBN 0-7603-0757-1 (pbk. : alk. paper)
      1. Steam locomotives–Conservation and
         restoration–United States. I. Title. II. Series

TJ603.4.U6 S65 2000
625.26'1'0973–dc21   00-028174

On the front cover: Southern Pacific No. 4449 works through the Sacramento River Canyon at Gibson, California. *Brian Solomon*

On the frontispiece: The drivers and rods on Nickel Plate Road 765 are a portrait of power. Nickel Plate's 2-8-4s featured 69-inch driving wheels, significantly larger than those used by the first Berkshires on the Boston & Albany, which were just 63 inches in diameter. *Brian Solomon*

On the table of contents page: Union Pacific 4-6-6-4 Challenger 3985 rests in Portola, California, in July 1992. *Brian Solomon*

On the title page: Milwaukee Road 4-8-4 No. 261, dressed up as Lackawanna No. 1661, rolls through Waukesha, Wisconsin, on October 11, 1994. *Brian Solomon*

On the back cover: Milwaukee Road S-3 4-8-4 No. 261 leads an excursion between Galesburg and Savanna, Illinois. *Brian Solomon*

C O N T E N T S

ACKNOWLEDGMENTS

One of the great pleasures of assembling a book like this one is looking at all the wonderful photographs that people have made of trains over the years. This book represents the efforts of many photographers, and I would like to thank everyone who lent me their work and photographs from their collections, especially the following: George C. Corey, Fred Matthews, William D. Middleton, Robert A. Buck, Tim Doherty, John Gruber, Brian Jennison, George Diamond, Robert W. Jones of Pine Tree Press, Russ Porter, Andrew Spieker, Vic Stone, J. R. Quinn, Doug Eisele, and James A. Speaker. I would like to thank my father, Richard Jay Solomon, for giving me unlimited access to his vast collection of photographs, timetables, and books. Many of the texts used to research this book are from his personal library. In addition, he assisted with photo research and proofreading. My brother Seán Solomon and mother Maureen Solomon have also helped in many ways over the years.

William Kratville of the Union Pacific Museum in Omaha, Nebraska, helped locate several photos, as did librarians at the Denver Public Library and California State Railroad Museum. Mike Gardner lent me the use of his darkroom and provided transportation on several steam quests.

It always helps to have experienced eyes review a text, so I thank George Corey, Robert A. Buck, and Harry Vallas for technical assistance and proofreading. Thanks also to Lee Klancher and Amy Glaser of MBI Publishing for their help in the editing and reviewing of the manuscript. I often travel with other photographers, and I thank all of them for their company and visual wisdom.

—*Brian Solomon, September 1999*

After 17 years of iron slumber in a Portland, Oregon, park, SP GS-4 4449 was resurrected and restored to service in 1975 to pull the American Freedom Train, a transcontinental display of artifacts of America's history commemorating the bicentennial. Following its duties, the 4449 led a cross-country Amtrak special back to Portland. Here the locomotive climbs SP's legendary Cuesta Hill north of San Luis Obispo, California, on April 27, 1977. *Brian Jennison*

American Steam

A steam locomotive is more than a machine; it is a personality.

—S. Kip Farrington, Jr.

The power of the locomotive changed America; allowing it to grow, prosper, and thrive. As railroads and America grew, railway traffic swelled. Trains grew heavier and longer, and passenger trains in particular moved faster and faster. Faster trains effectively shortened the distance between cities. A trip that had taken many days by horse and carriage was shortened to just hours. Speed also increased railway capacity because as trains moved faster, the railroad could handle more trains. Heavier, faster trains meant that railroads required increasingly

Under an enormous cloud of its own smoke, Southern Pacific's Lima-built Northern type, No. 4443, rolls through California's San Joaquin Valley on the West Side Line on March 24, 1957. *Fred Matthews*

9

A Baker valve gear arrangement on Chesapeake & Ohio 4-8-4 No. 614. Valve gear serves a function similar to a transmission on an automobile. It is made up of rods, eccentrics, and links, which the engineer uses to control the valves that direct the flow of steam to the cylinders, thus controlling the power and direction of the engine. Baker valve gear was one of several popular arrangements used on late-era steam locomotives. *Brian Solomon*

more powerful locomotives. From the time of the earliest railways in the 1820s and 1830s, locomotive builders worked to construct more powerful engines.

Traditionally, they obtained more power by building larger, heavier engines. The first locomotives were tiny, weighing just a few tons. For example, one of the earliest locomotives built in the United States, the *Best Friend of Charleston,* was an 0-4-0 type with 54-inch wheels that weighed just 4.5 tons (9,000 pounds). By the 1860s, American Standard was the

Chesapeake & Ohio No. 614 rolls across the Moodna Viaduct at Salisbury Mills, New York, on July 8, 1997. *Brian Solomon*

11

Late-era steam locomotive development produced advanced locomotive designs that were vastly more powerful than the first steam locomotives built a hundred years earlier. The cylinders, drive rods, and driving wheels on Southern Pacific 4-8-4 No. 4449 illustrate the great power of a modern steam locomotive. *Brian Solomon*

typical locomotive (a 4-4-0 wheel arrangement), weighing in the vicinity of 30 tons (60,000 pounds). By 1900, new locomotives often weighed as much as 200,000 pounds, and by 1910, huge, articulated locomotives, using a 2-8-8-2 wheel arrangement and weighing 430,000 pounds, were in daily service. As locomotives grew in size and weight, the railroads had to improve their tracks, bridges, right of ways, and servicing facilities to accommodate them. The heaviest, most powerful locomotives were often restricted to certain routes, as they were often too heavy, too long, and too tall for some portions of the railroad. As locomotive proportions grew, there was

Left
Southern Pacific GS-4 No. 4449 races toward Tehama, California, at Hooker Creek. *Brian Solomon*

Right
Southern Pacific GS-4 4449 leads an excursion across the Sacramento River at Reading, California, on September 1, 1991. *Brian Solomon*

On June 8, 1997, Chesapeake & Ohio 4-8-4 No. 614 raced through Port Jervis, New York. This locomotive is one of several large steam locomotives operating in excursion service in the United States. *Brian Solomon*

an ever increasing disparity between the mainline and secondary lines. The most powerful locomotives were usually of greatest value where they could do the most work, and that was usually on the mainline, while branch lines and secondary routes were often the bastion of older, lighter locomotives.

In the 1860s, the American Standard 4-4-0 worked both freight and passenger trains on the mainline, the branches, across the flatlands, and in the mountains, although specialized locomotives had been available since the beginning. In the 1840s, the Western Railroad of Massachusetts ordered a small fleet of 0-8-0s for heavy freight work in the Berkshire Hills. At that time, Western operated the longest stretch of steeply graded railway in the world, and its builders felt it required specialized locomotives with especially high tractive effort. By the 1890s, railway locomotives had become highly specialized machines, and some railroads used dozens of different classes of locomotives, each with a different intended application. For example, on some

A Canadian National 4-8-2 Mountain type catches a glint of the setting sun as it is being watered. CN operated a large fleet of 4-8-2s and was one of the first railroads to adopt the 4-8-4 wheel arrangement, essentially an expansion of the 4-8-2 type. *Donald Fellows*

lines fast mainline passenger locomotives would have used a 4-4-0 wheel arrangement with 78-inch drivers, while freight engines for slow mainline freight trains, known as "drags," used 2-8-0s with 51-inch drivers. However, at the end of the steam-building era in the late 1930s and 1940s, the trend had shifted back toward less-specialized locomotive designs. This continued into

Previous Page
In June 1996, the drive rods of Milwaukee Road 261 catch the sodium vapor glow from lamps at the diesel shop in Galesburg, Illinois. This powerful Northern-type steam locomotive was built during World War II when the War Production Board limited diesel production, encouraging railroads to acquire new steam power instead. Had it not been for the war, fewer lines would have purchased late-era steam power. Today Milwaukee Road 261 is maintained for mainline steam excursion service. *Brian Solomon*

the diesel era, and by the mid-1950s, only a few types of locomotives were being built for American railways.

Designing Locomotives

In an effort to obtain the best possible performance, American steam locomotives were specially designed to meet the needs of specific routes and applications. Each class of locomotives was usually customized and tailored to the purchasing railroad's specifications. The level of railroad involvement in locomotive design varied greatly. Some lines, such as the Pennsylvania Railroad and the Norfolk & Western, designed and built many of their own locomotives in company shops. Other lines worked closely with the established locomotive builders to develop a suitable design. Smaller railroads often relied on the builders to supply a suitable design. Locomotive

At 7 P.M. on July 30, 1958, a Norfolk & Western J Class 4-8-4 catches the glint of the setting sun at Roanoke, Virginia. The last steam locomotives were some of the finest machines ever made—a tribute to more than 125 years of development. The N&W J was capable of reaching speeds of up to 110 miles per hour. *Richard Jay Solomon*

costs were one of a railway's largest expenditures and, to keep costs down, it was extremely important to obtain optimum locomotive efficiency. How this was actually achieved varied greatly and reflected the independent and individual attitudes of each line's chief mechanical officer. No two railways had precisely the same approach, and each railway's operational differences affected its locomotive designs. As a result, many railroads were known for their distinctive motive power.

The locomotive's intended service, operating territory, and the quality of fuel and water it was to use all played a significant role in its design. To obtain maximum efficiency, many lines tried to design a locomotive that would closely match its intended service. An underpowered locomotive would not be able to meet schedules and might incur additional operation expenses if it needed extra helpers in graded territory or required "double heading" (the operation of two locomotives, each with its own crew) over the length of an entire district. It was more expensive to run two locomotives than one, so every effort was made to design a single locomotive that was powerful enough to handle average trains. However, if a locomotive was too big, too heavy, or too powerful, it could cost the railroad in a variety of other ways. A fleet of locomotives too big for the work needed represented a waste of resources.

Canadian National 4-8-4 No. 6218 leads an excursion across a bridge in Quebec in October 1964. *Richard Jay Solomon*

Big locomotives cost more to build than small ones, and no railway wanted to pay for more power than it required. More importantly if a locomotive was too heavy for the existing track structure, the line would require upgrading, which could be very expensive. There are instances of railroads building

locomotives that were too powerful for existing conditions.

The switch from wooden coaches to all-steel cars—which began around 1905 and was effectively complete for interstate service by about 1920—really pushed the limits of passenger locomotives.

18

An all-steel train was about 13 percent heavier than a wooden train of the same size and length. Not only did the cars become heavier, but during this same time, the trains grew much longer. In "Biography of a Heavy Pacific" (*Railroad History* 135), Robert Frey provided an example of passenger locomotive growth on the Northern Pacific over a 30-year period beginning in 1899, the period when passenger train weights and lengths increased most dramatically. Northern Pacific's Class N 4-4-2 Atlantics, built in 1899, weighed 126,800 pounds, used 19x26-inch cylinders (bore and stroke), had 78-inch driving wheels, operated with 180-psi boiler pressure, and produced 18,400 pounds of tractive effort. Its class Q-6 4-6-2 Pacifics weighed 278,800 pounds, used 26x28-inch cylinders and 73-inch drivers, operated at 200-psi boiler pressure, and produced 44,080 pounds tractive effort. Yet even this dramatic increase could not satisfy NP's growing passenger train weights, and in 1926 it produced a new wheel arrangement to obtain even greater power (see chapter 4).

Technological improvements, such as the development of high-tensile-strength alloy steels and refined precision machining techniques, plus innovations such as the application of roller bearings and the use of practical feed water heaters and front-end throttles, enabled locomotive designers to produce significantly more efficient steam locomotives than ever before. However, the most important innovation of the 1920s was the development of the weight-bearing, four-wheel trailing truck, which allowed for a dramatic increase in firebox and boiler dimensions. Ample boiler capacity provided the engine with greater power, which was converted into a greater tractive effort and higher sustained drawbar pull. However, a significantly larger firebox would not have been practical without the implementation of the mechanical stoker, which relieved the fireman of the burden of supplying the locomotive with coal by hand—a task requiring the movement of as much as

Milwaukee Road 261 rolls past ore docks at Duluth, Minnesota, on May 22, 1999. This handsome Alco-built 4-8-4 is one of several large steam locomotives that still operates in the United States. *John Gruber*

Santa Fe 3751 is the first Baldwin 4-8-4. It rolls through Redondo Junction, Los Angeles, California, in June 1999 on its way to the Sacramento Railfair. *Victor Stone*

four tons of coal an hour with a hand shovel. These improvements led to a whole new breed of vastly more powerful and efficient machines than had ever rolled before. They were the best and last steam locomotives. Their amount of raw power was awe-inspiring, but their tenure was short. Just a generation after the first superpower steam locomotives were built, they were gone. Another, more efficient form of power had taken their place.

Superpower Emerges

The modern locomotive is superior to old forms merely through the great power that enables it to decrease the payroll of train men engaged in the movement of a given volume of freight.

—Angus Sinclair

Opportunity spawns innovation, and newcomers in business often take advantage of an idea that established businesses have overlooked. Lima Locomotive Works did just that in the early 1920s. Lima was the newest and smallest of the three large

Although built to haul freight, Nickel Plate Road 2-8-4 No. 765 has enjoyed a long and productive career as an excursion engine. In July 1989, No. 765 was used to haul a series of trips around Buffalo, New York. It is seen approaching Black Rock on its return from Niagara Falls on July 2, 1989. *Brian Solomon*

In the mid-1950s, the Pennsylvania Railroad borrowed steam power from the Santa Fe. On August 10, 1956, Santa Fe 5034, a 2-10-4 Texas type, leads a 101-car-long Pennsylvania Railroad coal train from Columbus to Sandusky over the Baltimore & Ohio crossing at Attica Junction, Ohio. *George Diamond*

commercial locomotive builders and needed an edge to get ahead, so it bucked convention to build a better steam engine.

While the modern company known as Lima Locomotive Works had existed only since 1916, its roots dated back to 1869. Its predecessors had been building specialized geared locomotives called Shays since 1880, and began building full-sized locomotives in 1911.

Thus in the 1920s, Lima was a newcomer to the large locomotive business compared to the established giants of Baldwin and Alco. At that time, Baldwin was among the largest locomotive builders in the world. It was founded in 1831 by a Philadelphia

watchmaker/machinist named Matthias Baldwin. The American Locomotive Company (Alco) was formed in 1901 when a number of independent locomotive manufacturers joined forces to better compete with Baldwin. Some of these companies dated back to the first half of the nineteenth century. Baldwin and Alco represented the vast majority of new locomotive orders, leaving Lima with a small share of the business. In order to command a larger portion of this lucrative manufacturing business, Lima's engineers set out to design a better locomotive.

Following World War I, American railroads were faced with growing freight traffic and increased competition. By the early 1920s, private

The Nickel Plate Road was among the last American railroads to give up on steam; it was still ordering new Berkshires as late as 1949. But a decade later it was facing the prospect of dieselization and its Berkshires were working off their last revenue miles. In January 1958, Nickel Plate Road 2-8-4 No. 751 is serviced at Calumet, Illinois. *Russ Porter*

automobiles had severely cut into passenger traffic, and competition from trucks on the highway had begun to erode the railroad's freight traffic. Passenger trains were at the forefront of public attention, but railroads earned most of their money from freight traffic. While the railroads were carrying more freight, they were losing market share. Some traffic, such as less-than-carload traffic (small shipments), was in severe decline as trucks stole away the business.

Traditionally, railroads had improved passenger services by providing better equipment and operating faster schedules. In the 1830s, passenger trains typically operated at just 10 to 15 miles per hour and rarely exceeded 25 miles per hour. But by the 1920s, many lines were regularly running trains

at 70 to 80 miles per hour and faster. Train names often expressed speed: *The Exposition Flyer, Wabash Cannonball, Empire State Express,* and the *Fast Mail*.

Freight, despite its greater revenues, had not enjoyed the increase of train speeds. In the early 1920s, freights still plodded along, averaging about 10 to 12 miles per hour—not much faster than the primitive trains of the 1830s. Until then there had been little incentive to move freight faster. The only competition for freight trains had been water transportation and horse-drawn wagons on rutted dirt roads, and both were much slower than freight trains. Since faster trains required more fuel and resulted in a higher cost, the railroads were reluctant to operate fast freight and were quite content with slow-speed "drags"—long, heavy trains. As a

In the 1920s, Alco promoted the three-cylinder simple locomotive as a way of obtaining greater power from a nonarticulated engine. The third cylinder was located below the smoke box between the two outside cylinders and drove a cranked axle. The largest three-cylinder locomotives were a fleet of 88 4-12-2s built for Union Pacific between 1926 and 1930. These were also the largest American locomotives with a rigid frame and were designated the Union Pacific type. Union Pacific 4-12-2 No. 9051 rests at Omaha, Nebraska, in 1954. *Union Pacific Museum Collection*

result, freight locomotives were designed as slow-moving, high-tractive-effort machines. In the World War I era, freight power was typically 2-8-0 Consolidations, 2-8-2 Mikados, 2-10-2 Santa Fes, and large powerful Mallet Compounds—locomotives known for their great power, but not speed.

When trucks began to snatch lucrative freight traffic away from the rails, a market for fast freight locomotives developed. Suddenly the plodding 2-10-2s and Mallets that had been all the rage during World War I were just not fast enough. Passenger locomotives were designed for speed, but they were intended to move comparatively light trains (600 to 1,000 tons).

To meet the need for faster and more powerful locomotives, several developmental approaches were tried. Alco promoted three-cylinder simple engines and the Mallet compound was modified into a simple articulated design (see chapter 5). But the most successful solution was Lima's superpower concept, which did not involve significantly more complex machinery or a substantially larger locomotive to achieve a dramatic power increase.

In his time, William Woodard was one of the foremost locomotive designers in the United States. He had worked for both Alco and Baldwin before going to work for Lima in 1916. At Lima, he directed the company's efforts toward building better locomotives and his visionary designs were vastly more efficient than anything previously built, influencing the entire locomotive industry.

Woodard was convinced that if he designed better locomotives, Lima would secure a larger share of the locomotive market, and he was right. His basic concept was fairly straightforward, yet it ran contrary to industry trends. Instead of just building a bigger, heavier locomotive, he intended to build a more powerful one that gave significantly better performance without a dramatic weight increase. This would allow railroads to haul more tonnage without having to spend money upgrading their lines.

One of Lima's best customers was the New York Central, one of the largest railroads in the United States and consequently one of the largest consumers of new locomotives. New York Central was pleased with Lima's early products and was very interested in fast freight. Its four-track mainline between New York and Chicago via Buffalo, New York, known as the Water Level Route, was one of the busiest corridors for both freight and passenger traffic in the United States. Using its 4-8-2 Mohawks, New York Central became one of the pioneers of fast freight. Central's concept was to move trains of traditional length faster, rather than just moving bigger trains. Instead of using the 4-8-2 and 2-8-2 to pull a heavier train, Central applied the power to run the same size trains faster. It was successful, and by the early 1920s, Central was looking to expand fast freight service across its system.

One area that presented difficulties for New York Central was its heavily graded Boston & Albany route, which connected its namesake cities by a rugged crossing of the Berkshire Hills in western Massachusetts. This was the old Western Railroad of Massachusetts route that had required some of the first specialized locomotives. While eighty years had passed since the first Winans 0-8-0 "Mud Diggers" had crawled up through the Berkshires, this route still presented a formidable crossing, as it does today. These were the longest, toughest mainline grades on New York Central and some of the few places

On a rainy autumn day in 1968, Nickel Plate Road No. 759 leads an excursion west of Albany, New York. This locomotive worked in excursion service until the early 1970s. Although no longer in working order, No. 759 is part of the Steamtown collection in Scranton, Pennsylvania. *Richard Jay Solomon*

where the railroad operated Mallet compounds and 2-10-2 Santa Fes.

In the early 1920s, the 2-8-2 Mikado was the standard workhorse of the American railroad. New York Central employed hundreds of them, and thousands were working freight duties all around the nation. Statistically, you were more likely to

The Erie Railroad was the first line to use Berkshires capable of high-speed freight operation. Its 2-8-4s used 69-inch drivers, instead of the 63-inch drivers used on the original A-1 Berkshire. The Erie was one of several railways under control of the Van Swerigan brothers, and Erie's Berkshires set a precedent for motive power design on the other Van Swerigan lines. A Baldwin-built S-3 2-8-4 leads a freight out of Erie's East Hornell, New York, yards. *John Long, Erie Railroad, Tim Doherty collection*

encounter a Mikado than just about any other type of engine. In 1922, Woodard approached the New York Central with his advanced locomotive designs and persuaded the railroad to order an experimental 2-8-2 Mikado based on Central's successful H-7e 2-8-2 design. The H-7e was a contemporary Alco product built in the autumn of 1920 that featured 63-inch drivers, 27x30-inch cylinders, and a 60-square-foot firebox grate. It worked at 200 pounds boiler pressure, weighed 328,000 pounds, and produced 59,000 pounds tractive effort. It was intended for

heavy freight work and represented a remarkably more powerful locomotive than earlier designs. But like the more powerful locomotives of the period, it was also significantly heavier than the locomotives it replaced.

In 1922, Lima delivered its H-10 Mikado prototype, which featured only a nominal weight increase over the H-7e design: at 334,000 pounds it was just 3 tons (6,000 pounds) heavier, an increase of only 1.8 percent. Yet the H-10's trailing truck booster was able to produce 74,500 pounds tractive effort, 25 percent more power than the H-7e. In service, New York Central found that the H-10 could haul freight at 30 to 35 miles per hour—more than twice the speed of its conventional Mikados. The H-10's ability to race tonnage along at sustained speed mile after mile set it apart from all other freight locomotives. In the eyes of the New York Central, Lima had built a real winner.

The H-10's cylinders were slightly larger than those of the H-7e (28x30 inches), and the firebox grate was expanded to 66 square feet, but other basic locomotive specifications had remained essentially the same, including driving wheels and boiler pressure. What made the H-10 a substantially more powerful and efficient engine was its larger firebox and other efficiencies gained through a variety of modern equipment and innovations.

Recent advancements in steel making had made a variety of new high-tensile-strength alloy steels available at reasonable cost. New microscopic photography techniques allowed for higher quality control. Alloy steels were not new (the U.S. Navy had been using nickel steel as armor plating on ships since 1891), but now they were cost effective for locomotive construction, and the H-10 was one of the first to take advantage of this improvement. Heat-treated chrome vanadium steel was used for reciprocating parts, including side and main rods.

The H-10 employed an improved type of steam superheater that was more efficient than earlier designs. Instead of a conventional steam injector, the H-10 introduced water to the boiler using an Elesco feedwater heater. Feedwater heaters were nothing new; pioneer locomotive designer Richard Trevithick—credited for building one of the earliest steam locomotives in England—is said to have invented one in 1803. Yet, they were not commonly used until after World War I. A feedwater heater conserves energy by using exhaust steam to preheat water entering the boiler. Many conventional methods of pumping water from the tender into the boiler did not heat the water, and introducing cool water to the boiler would reduce average boiler water temperature resulting in a temporary loss of power and greater fuel consumption.

The H-10's efficiency was further improved by the use of an external dry pipe and front-end throttle, which gave the locomotive engineer better control of the steam as it left the boiler and aided in fuel efficiency. The H-10 used a booster that would be activated by the locomotive engineer. The booster was an auxiliary steam engine designed to engage the trailing truck axle at slow speeds to generate additional power for starting a train. This device was especially valuable for overcoming inertia when starting long, heavy trains.

New York Central was especially pleased with the H-10 and ordered 302 of them—an enormous order for a single type. As good as it was, the H-10 was just an evolutionary improvement of the 2-8-2 design. However, it was a step toward the development of the 2-8-4, a truly groundbreaking machine, which had great influence on future locomotive designs. Incidentally, while Lima secured a portion of New York Central's H-10 order—it built 115 of them—the larger portion of the order was awarded to New York Central's regular builder, Alco. New York Central's disproportionate allocation of the order may seem odd by today's standards, but Lima was still probably fairly pleased with the outcome. An order for 115 new H-10 locomotives cost New York Central about $8.3 million, and that was a lot of money in 1922. If Lima had not originated the design, it probably wouldn't have secured an order for nearly that many new locomotives from New York Central. New York Central assigned eight Alco-built H-10a 2-8-2s to freight service on the rugged Boston & Albany line and they excelled in this service.

The Berkshire

In 1924, Lima's Woodard set out to improve upon the H-10 design and build an even more

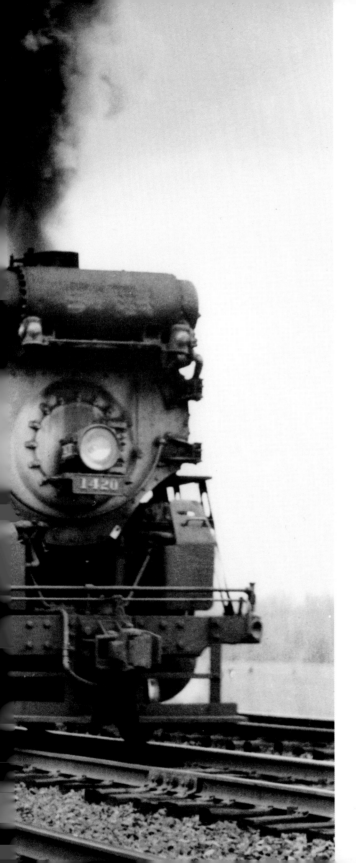

powerful locomotive. Woodard hoped to improve efficiency by 10 to 20 percent. The locomotive that Lima built under his direction was unlike anything ever seen on an American railroad before. It featured a distinctive wheel arrangement (2-8-4) and was one of the first locomotives ever built with a weight bearing two-axle trailing truck. To highlight the new locomotive's superlative potential, it was designated A-1. The secret behind the A-1 was a significantly larger firebox grate and ample boiler capacity, combined with a host of efficient devices such as those demonstrated on the highly successful H-10.

To demonstrate the prototype, Lima went to New York Central's vast new Selkirk Yard, south of Albany, New York. This large freight yard is a base of operation for freight service on the Boston & Albany route (as well as other freight routes south and west of Albany). Here the A-1 would be able to show off on the toughest terrain New York Central had to offer. The Lima A-1 weighed 390,000 pounds, but despite its enormous 100-square-foot firebox (more than a third larger than that used on the H-10), it placed only 1 percent greater weight on drivers. The remainder of the excess weight was carried by the two-axle trailing truck.

The A-1, which was only nominally heavier than the H-10 and used the same-size drivers and 28x30-inch cylinders, could haul a heavier train significantly faster. Its secret was a high-capacity boiler that provided ample steam to maintain higher speed and a 60 percent cylinder cutoff, which limited steam admission into the cylinders, allowing for greater

Boston & Albany's A-1 Berkshire 1420 leads a freight through Weston Park, Massachusetts, in September 1936. Lima's 2-8-4 Berkshire influenced most subsequent steam locomotive designs. In addition to the four-wheel trailing truck, the Berkshire employed a variety of energy-saving appliances, including an Elesco Feedwater Heater—the prominent horizontal cylinder above the headlight. *J. R. Quinn collection.*

The secret to the Berkshire's success was its large firebox and ample boiler, which allowed the engine to haul heavy tonnage at sustained speeds without running out of steam. In 1938, a 12-year-old Lima-built A-1 Berkshire leads a freight through Englishman's Curve at East Chatham, New York, on the west end of the Boston & Albany line. It was on this piece of railroad that Lima's first 2-8-4 demonstrated its abilities in 1925. *J. R. Quinn collection*

In February 1958, a Nickel Plate Road 2-8-4 Berkshire leads a westbound freight through Hobart, Indiana. The last steam locomotive built by Lima was Nickel Plate 2-8-4 No. 779. It was constructed in 1949, roughly 25 years after Lima had introduced the type with its famous A-1. *Russ Porter*

expansion and more efficient steam usage and therefore lower fuel consumption. Where older types might run out of steam hauling a heavy train, the A-1 had plenty of steam for the heaviest train New York Central could put together, and it could maintain a steady speed up the steepest grades on the B&A. The A-1 was notable for its utilitarian appearance. The front end prominently featured an Elesco feedwater heater, an oversized boiler that rose to meet the roofline of the cab, and an excess of piping and accessories, making for a surly, businesslike machine. This locomotive was clearly built to haul heavy freight.

New York Central staged an event where an H-10 left Selkirk eastbound on the B&A with a typical freight. An hour or so later, the A-1 followed hauling a slightly heavier train. The A-1 was so much more powerful than the H-10 that within 50 miles of leaving the yard, the A-1 had overtaken the slower moving 2-8-2, thus demonstrating its fantastic power. The 2-8-4 was a vastly superior machine and a true leap in steam technology. It was the very first "superpowered" steam locomotive—the term Lima coined for its new design—and the first of a new generation of steam locomotives.

The 2-8-4 was designated the Berkshire type in honor of the hills where its ability was demonstrated. New York Central was extremely impressed with its performance and placed an order with Lima for 25 2-8-4s, which it classed A-1. These were delivered in 1926, followed by an order for 20 more 2-8-4s in 1927, and a third order in 1930 for 10 more. The third order, class A-1c, featured an improved appearance and was known among operating crews as the "sports model." The Berkshires ruled the B&A's line for two decades, and they quickly caught on around the country. Illinois Central purchased the A-1 prototype and ordered a fleet of 50 nearly identical 2-8-4s from Lima. A number of other lines also adopted the 2-8-4. Boston & Albany's Berkshires were considered fast mountain climbers but were allowed to operate only at 35 to 40 miles per hour. Later Berkshires, such as those used on the Nickel Plate Road, featured taller drivers and regularly worked at 70 miles per hour on fast freight.

The Texas Type

The success of the 2-8-4 prompted Woodard to expand his successful formula into a 10-coupled design. This would provide a locomotive with even greater tractive effort while still maintaining reasonable axle loading. So in 1925, even before the first production 2-8-4s were delivered to the Boston & Albany, Lima built a 2-10-4 type for the Texas & Pacific. It was named for the T&P and is known as the Texas type—a fitting name for such a large machine. This was not the very first application of this wheel arrangement—the Santa Fe had built an experimental locomotive using this arrangement a few years earlier—but earlier 10-coupled types (the 2-10-0 Decapod and 2-10-2 Santa Fe) suffered from

Chesapeake & Ohio was the first railroad to use 2-10-4s with tall drivers. Its 40 2-10-4s, built by Lima in 1930, class T-1, were an adaptation of the Erie 2-8-4 and are considered some of the best Texas types ever made. They inspired Pennsylvania's famous J Class 2-10-4s, which were built during World War II. A C&O 2-10-4 and a 2-6-6-6 Allegheny lead an empty coal train at Henderson Road on the north side of Columbus, Ohio, about 1950. *Andrew M. Spieker*

The Central Vermont Railway operated 10 2-10-4s built by Alco in 1928. They were the smallest Texas types ever built, weighing just 419,000 pounds, but they were the largest steam locomotives in New England. On February 2, 1948, Central Vermont No. 701 leads a northbound freight through the train shed at Essex Junction, Vermont. *Philip R. Hastings, Tim Doherty collection*

Color photographs of the Chicago Great Western—a Granger line that connected Chicago, the Twin Cities, Council Bluffs, and Kansas City—are rare, but even more rare are action shots of its big steam. One of CGW's big 2-10-4 Texas types leads a freight near Kidder, Iowa. *Leon Onofri collection, courtesy of Robert W. Jones*

problems that had limited their service application and popularity. Both types were built with relatively small drivers and were intended for slow-speed drag freight service. The reason for this was simple: the enormous piston thrust required to power the locomotive placed great stress on its frame and cylinders. Also, the locomotive's small driving wheels were difficult to counterbalance properly, and therefore tended to exhibit exceptionally high dynamic augment, which pounded the tracks and stressed locomotive components. Furthermore, 10-coupled locomotives required larger cylinders and used more steam than smaller locomotives and, as a result, would tend to exhaust conventional boiler capacity when moving at speed.

Woodard addressed these problems with the Texas type. His large boiler provided the 2-10-4 with ample steam to maintain speed with a heavy train. Texas & Pacific's 2-10-4s were remarkably similar to the A-1, and they shared a common appearance, including the prominent Elesco feedwater heater on the front of the engine. Like the Berkshire, they used 63-inch drivers and a 100-square-foot firebox grate. The 2-10-4's boiler pressure was slightly higher, 250 psi compared to 240 psi on the 2-8-4, and its cylinders were larger, measuring 29x32 inches. While the 2-10-4 weighed 448,000 pounds, roughly 63,000 pounds more than the A-1, its axle loading was roughly the same: 60,000 pounds for the 2-10-4 and 62,050 for the 2-8-4. Lightweight reciprocating parts helped the Texas type overcome some of the dynamic augment difficulties faced by 2-10-2s.

It is no surprise that Texas & Pacific was extremely pleased with the Lima design, and it ultimately bought 70 of them. The type was further refined in 1930 when Chesapeake & Ohio expanded a Berkshire design used by the Erie and developed the first high-drivered Texas type. Tall wheels allowed for better counterbalancing and reduced the number of wheel rotations per mile. This further

minimized dynamic augment, allowing for much higher speeds. The Santa Fe ordered some of the largest 2-10-4s, enormous machines with 74-inch drivers, 30x34-inch cylinders (among the largest ever used by a simple engine), 310-pound boiler pressure, and a total engine weight (minus tender) of 545,000 pounds. The locomotive delivered an impressive 93,000-pound tractive effort and produced 5,600 drawbar horsepower at 40 miles per hour. But the locomotive's most impressive statistic was the incredible piston thrust, an estimated 210,000 pounds, the greatest of any locomotive ever built.

The Pennsylvania Railroad operated the largest fleet of Texas types, which were also the heaviest ever built. There is a certain technological irony in this statistic because Pennsylvania had its own distinctive ideas about motive power and resisted investment in superpower steam during the 1920s and 1930s. Instead it followed a unique path, first choosing to refine and construct its own more conventional steam designs, while simultaneously pursuing an aggressive mainline electrification program, which released large numbers of older engines for service elsewhere on the railroad. Then in the mid-1930s, PRR embarked on a plan to develop the Duplex type and continued to ignore many contemporary designs.

During World War II, PRR suffered from a severe motive power shortage and planned to build a fleet of passenger and freight Duplex types. However, the War Production Board prevented PRR from constructing these unusual designs and insisted that PRR adapt an existing locomotive type. It was this directive that forced PRR to adopt the 2-10-4 using the highly successful C&O Texas type for a model. Many steam authorities believe that PRR's Class J 2-10-4s were the finest steam locomotives ever operated by the railroad, and they were certainly much more successful than PRR's Duplex types that were constructed after the war .

Hudsons

. . . it has been our endeavor for succeeding reciprocating steam designs steadily to decrease weight per horsepower developed and to increase the steam gener- ating plant and drawbar pull capacities and over-all thermal efficiencies.

—Paul Kiefer
from *A Practical Evaluation of Railroad Motive Power*

The 4-6-4 Hudson type was born out of New York Central's need for a more powerful, faster pas- senger locomotive. New York Central's Paul Kiefer, one of its top locomotive designers, dreamed up the Hudson by expanding on Central's Pacific type idea

Canadian Pacific's semistreamlined Hudsons were adorned with royal crowns after 4-6-4 2850 hauled England's King George VI and Queen Elizabeth across Canada in 1939. The crown insignia can be seen at the front of the locomotive above the cylinders. Royal Hudson 2827 pauses for inspection at London, Ontario, in November 1959. *Andrew M. Spieker*

35

New York Central J-1 Hudson 5328 leads the *North Shore Limited* through Tivoli, New York, in September 1949. The locomotive is taking water from a track pan located between the rails. New York Central was one of a few lines that used track pans to speed up operations. On most lines, steam locomotives had to stop at regular intervals to fill the tender. *William D. Middleton*

and enlarged the firebox and boiler. The larger firebox was supported using the four-wheel rear trailing truck developed on the successful Berkshire type. Since the Hudson was intended as a passenger locomotive, New York Central felt that its premier passenger trains should be hauled by a machine that not only performed well but looked good, so Kiefer worked with Alco to design a balanced, aesthetically pleasing machine.

Prototype 4-6-4, class J-1a, No. 5200 was delivered in February 1927 and was named in honor of the mighty Hudson River, which New York Central followed for miles on its run from New York City to Albany. It was a magnificent locomotive and featured 79-inch drivers, 25x28-inch cylinders, an 81.5-square-foot firebox grate (roughly 20 percent larger than the New York Central's most modern Pacific), and operated at 225-psi boiler pressure. Like the Berkshire, the Hudson used a variety of modern energy conserving appliances. However, auxiliary plumbing such as the Elesco feedwater heater was not exposed—as on the first Berkshires—but neatly

covered beneath the boiler jacketing to satisfy Kiefer's aesthetic concerns.

Kiefer's Hudson was enormously successful. It was significantly more powerful than the railroad's best Pacific, and New York Central ordered a great fleet; 205 J-1s were built between 1927 and 1931. Later J-1s featured a variety of improvements over earlier passenger power such as Baker valve gear, cast-steel frames, and larger tenders.

Refined Hudsons

In the 1930s, New York Central refined its Hudson design into one of the finest machines ever to roll on American rails. These improved machines, known as J-3as, were truly super locomotives and featured a variety of improvements. The piston stroke was shortened to 22.5 inches, the cylinder bore increased by 1 inch to 29 inches, and boiler pressure was raised to 275 psi. Aluminum was used for running boards, cabs, and other nonessential equipment to limit the total weight of the locomotive, while alloy steel was used for piston rods, main

On a frigid winter morning, a New York Central Hudson departs Harmon, New York, with a long passenger train from Grand Central Station. This train has just exchanged its electric locomotive for steam, as all trains used electric power between Grand Central and Harmon. The electric third rail is seen adjacent to the tracks in the foreground. *Tim Doherty collection*

The two primary Canadian railways had very different philosophies toward modern steam power. The Canadian Pacific preferred six-coupled power and operated many 4-6-2 Pacifics and 4-6-4 Hudsons, while Canadian National preferred eight-coupled locomotives, operating the largest fleet of 4-8-4s in North America. An exception to this rule were five Canadian National 4-6-4 Hudsons built by the Montreal Locomotive Works in 1930. Don Fellows caught CN 4-6-4 No. 5702 in Quebec on October 5, 1958. *Donald Fellows*

rods, and other reciprocating parts for reduced dynamic augment, which was especially severe when operating at high speeds. Instead of traditional spoked driving wheels, the Hudsons used Boxpok and Scullin Disc designs (advanced wheel designs). Timken roller bearings were employed on all of the J-3's wheels and tenders. These combined improvements proved extremely effective. The J-3a produced a maximum of 4,725 horsepower at 75 miles per hour; 875 more horsepower than produced by the J-1. Furthermore the J-3a used less coal and water than J-1s and exhibited one of the best reliability and service records of any New York Central locomotive. J-1s regularly ran more than 20,000 miles per month hauling the "Great Steel Fleet"—the name for New York Central's extensive long distance passenger train network.

New York Central was enormously proud of its Hudsons and used them to advertise the railroad at every opportunity. They were featured on timetables, posters, and in magazine ads. Unfortunately,

this pride did not last. After diesels took over and New York Central bumped Hudsons from premier runs, some 4-6-4s ended their service working freight, all of the Hudsons were retired, and every last one was cut up for scrap. Not one example was preserved for posterity, a shame considering that the New York Central Hudson represented one of the greatest technological achievements of modern times.

While New York Central originated the 4-6-4, perfected it, and owned more than half of all the 4-6-4s built for service in North America, it was not the only railroad to run 4-6-4s. The Nickel Plate Road was quick to adopt the type and its first 4-6-4s, which used smaller drivers than the J-1 (just 73 inches), were in service only months after New York Central's first Hudson. Santa Fe also adopted the 4-6-4 for passenger service and ordered 10 4-6-4s from Baldwin in 1927. But, other than these early orders and New York Central's fleet, the Hudson was relatively slow to catch on.

The first steam locomotives built as streamliners were a pair of Milwaukee Road 4-4-2 Atlantics constructed in 1935 for high-speed service on the *Hiawatha*. The shrouds were designed by Otto Kuhler to reduce wind resistance and improve the appearance of the engine. Two additional streamlined Atlantics followed suit in 1936 and 1937. In addition to these pioneers, Milwaukee Road also ordered new streamlined 4-6-4s and applied shrouds to older 4-6-2s and 4-6-0s. Milwaukee Road No. 1, the first streamlined Atlantic, is seen at Caledonia, Wisconsin, in May 1951. *Russ Porter*

More 4-6-4s

Milwaukee Road had drawn up plans for a 4-6-4 before New York Central. However, financial constraints forced Milwaukee to postpone building its 4-6-4, letting New York Central steal the show. In 1929, Milwaukee Road finally ordered a fleet of 14 high-drivered 4-6-4s from Baldwin for fast passenger service. While in its early plans Milwaukee Road called the 4-6-4 a Milwaukee type, it usually referred to its 4-6-4s as Baltics, which is what the 4-6-4 was

Detail of the streamlined Chesapeake & Ohio 4-6-4 No. 490, featuring stainless-steel trim, headlights, and number board. *Brian Solomon*

called in Europe. Some authorities argue that the difference between a Hudson and a Baltic is defined by the wheel sizes on the trailing truck; one set of the Hudson's wheels is smaller than the other, while a Baltic uses wheels of the same size. Regardless, both

Left

After New York Central, Canadian Pacific was the second-largest user of the 4-6-4 in North America. On August 23, 1958, Royal Hudson 2821 leads a scheduled passenger train near St. Luc Junction in Montreal. *Richard Jay Solomon*

Hudsons and Baltics feature the 4-6-4 wheel arrangement and were used in essentially the same type of service. Milwaukee ordered an additional eight Baldwin 4-6-4s in 1931 and six streamlined 4-6-4s from Alco in 1938, which are considered among the best of the type ever built.

Canadian Pacific also adopted the 4-6-4 in 1929 and came to operate one of the largest fleets of Hudsons in North America, which totaled 65 locomotives. CP's last 4-6-4s were by far its most famous.

In 1946 and 1947, Chesapeake & Ohio rebuilt five 4-6-2 Pacifics into modern 4-6-4 Hudsons. They featured roller bearings and rotary cam poppet valves. Four received distinctive stainless-steel shrouding. One locomotive was preserved, and it is one of only a handful of American streamlined steam locomotives that escaped the scrap heap. Today it is displayed at the Baltimore & Ohio Railroad Museum in Baltimore, Maryland. *Brian Solomon*

They were semi-streamlined engines, class H1, built by the Montreal Locomotive Works between 1937 and 1940, and were known as Royal Hudsons because two of their class hauled the special trains carrying King George VI and Queen Elizabeth across Canada in 1939. All of the Royal Hudsons were decorated with an embossed royal crown.

Chesapeake & Ohio adopted the Hudson type much later than other lines, not ordering any until 1941. However, it remained loyal to the type later than most other American railroads and had the distinction of buying the very last 4-6-4s built in North America. These were extremely modern machines that featured a variety of state-of-the-art components including roller bearings, lightweight reciprocating gear, and Franklin poppet valves instead of conventional piston valves. They were also the heaviest and the most powerful Hudsons ever built. While they provided superlative service, they also had some of the shortest careers of any successful new steam locomotives and were retired in the mid-1950s after just a few years of service. Many Hudsons suffered early retirement because, despite their modern design, they could not compete with new passenger diesels. Since most 4-6-4s were specially designed for fast passenger service, they were not well suited for other work. So while some served as freight locomotives for a short time, they were swiftly retired in favor of other locomotives, including much older steam locomotives.

"My youth was charmed by the glamour of the locomotive."

—Raymond Loewy

Styled streamlined trains emerged in the 1930s, coincident with a world-wide streamlining movement that affected most transportation modes. Locomotive streamlining had two potential advantages: better performance and a more pleasing appearance. Because aerodynamic streamlining reduced air resistance, railroads interested in high-speed operation often considered streamlined designs a necessity for better performance. Yet the driving force for many streamlined steam designs was not the promise of improved performance, but better aesthetics.

In December 1934, New York Central applied streamlined, wind-resistant shrouds on to the J-1 Hudson No. 5344, Commodore Vanderbilt. The first steam locomotives built as streamliners were high-speed 4-4-2 Atlantics built by Alco for Milwaukee Road. They wore colorful shrouds designed by Otto Kuhler. Milwaukee went on to order new

One of the largest fleets of streamlined steam locomotives was Pennsylvania Railroad's unusual T1 Duplexes. These locomotives featured two complete sets of running gear on a rigid frame and were designed for 100-miles-per-hour operation. PRR T1 is portrayed in a World War II–era advertisement. *Author collection*

streamlined 4-6-4s and also streamlined a number of older locomotives using Kuhler-inspired shrouds. By the late 1930s, many railroads were ordering streamlined locomotives or dressing up older power, and many of these designs were the work of Otto Kuhler and his contemporaries, Raymond Loewy and Henry Dreyfuss.

One of the largest users of streamlined steam was the Pennsylvania Railroad, with its unique fleet of divided-drive Duplexes, class T1. These powerful, fast, Loewy-styled locomotives used two sets of cylinders and running gear on a rigid frame to reduce dynamic augment and the length of the piston thrust. Capable of hauling a 1,000-ton train at a sustained 100 miles per hour, they are known to have hit speeds in excess of 120 miles per hour. Unfortunately, the T1s were fraught with technical problems and didn't fare well when faced with modern diesels.

Northerns

. . . locomotive operation is the fundamental element in rail transportation.

—John W. Barringer, from *Super-Railroads.*

It's an unusually still evening. Ice crystals hang in the air and the snow covering the cornfields adjacent to New York Central's four-track mainline radiates a cool lunar glow. New York Central's famous Water Level Route runs from Grand Central Terminal in Manhattan to Chicago. It's primarily a low-grade route, but the short climb from Bergen to Batavia up the Niagara Escarpment on the way to Buffalo is often overlooked. It's just a slight grade, enough to make most westward trains work a little harder and, on rare occasion, cause some underpowered freights to stall. The railroad has been quiet for nearly three-quarters of an hour, but it is about to come to life. The flagship *Twentieth Century Limited*—one of the most recognized trains in the world—is

Union Pacific 844 leads a short freight westbound at Grand Island, Nebraska, in September 1996. This Union Pacific Northern type is one of the most traveled steam locomotives operating today. It was the last built in an order of 10 4-8-4s from Alco in 1944. *Brian Solomon*

45

due. There's a grade here, but this train won't be delayed in the slightest. The road has been cleared and the train is powered by a brand-new 4-8-4 Niagara, a locomotive with more power in its boiler than anything else on the line. The rails begin to vibrate and the yellow glow of the headlight makes the snow brighter. Then the huge machine shatters the winter silence as it races past at 80 miles per hour with 20 streamlined Pullmans in tow. The succinct bark of its exhaust reveals that it is working but not straining. This is one of the most advanced and powerful steam locomotives ever designed, and it is not yet one year old. It races toward Batavia, toward Buffalo, and on to Chicago. New York Central's strategically placed track pans will alleviate the need for water stops, and this locomotive will complete its demanding run on time, despite its unusually heavy consist. The Niagara is a tribute to the power of New York Central and its designer, Paul Kiefer. While New York Central was one of the last railroads to develop the 4-8-4, its Niagaras were some of the finest 4-8-4s and indeed some of the finest locomotives ever conceived.

This night in 1947, 4-8-4s are hauling some of the best-known trains in North America. On Southern Pacific, a streamlined GS-4, a 1941 product of Lima, leads an 18-car *Lark* down the Coast Line between San Francisco and Los Angeles. SP's *Lark* is the West Coast equivalent of Central's *Twentieth Century*. It is an all-Pullman sleeper train that connects California's two largest cities, and only the railroad's finest locomotives are entrusted with its run. The GS-4 is a superlative example of

One of New York Central's magnificent Niagaras leads a long passenger train northward (railroad timetable west) along the Hudson River at Oscawanna, New York. These locomotives epitomized late-era steam, featuring high-capacity boilers, lightweight alloy steel reciprocating parts, roller bearings on all axles, and exceptional reliability. A new S-1 Niagara, as seen here, cost New York Central nearly $240,000 in 1945. *Tim Doherty collection*

47

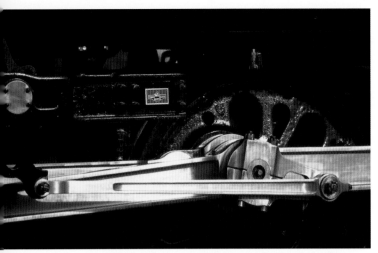

In 1930, Timken promoted the use of its tapered roller bearings by ordering a special locomotive fully equipped with them. This stunt changed railroad industry's attitude toward roller bearings and today most locomotives and rolling stock are so equipped. Many late-era steam locomotives used Timken bearings, as evidenced on Milwaukee Road 261. Roller bearings increased efficiency and greatly reduced the chance of a bearing failure. *Brian Solomon*

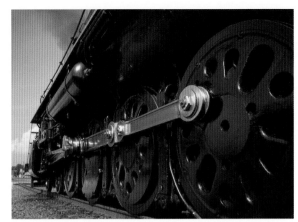

Milwaukee Road 261 is a thoroughly modern steam locomotive featuring lightweight drivers and reciprocation parts, as well as roller bearings on all axles, and a large high-capacity boiler. *Brian Solomon*

the 4-8-4 type, and this one sports SP's handsome daylight colors (yellow, orange, black, and silver), designed to match the train of the same name. At the same time, a Northern Pacific 4-8-4 leads the *North Coast Limited* west across North Dakota. While the 4-8-4 is known by a host of names, it is most certainly a Northern on Northern Pacific.

The NP was the first road to use the 4-8-4 and gave it the controversial name, Northern. Why is this a controversy? Because no other locomotive type has ever carried more names than the 4-8-4. Many lines adopted NP's Northern, but many others applied their own moniker. On the Lackawanna they were known as Poconos, while the nearby Lehigh Valley called them Wyomings. For a while, Canadian National called them Confederations; the Nashville, Chattanooga & St. Louis referred to its 4-8-4s as Dixies; and Chesapeake & Ohio called them Greenbriers.

The 4-8-4 was initially conceived as a passenger locomotive on NP, but some lines used it primarily as a freight engine, and on many lines it served as a dual-service locomotive. No other modern locomotive was better suited for a dual-service application than the 4-8-4. Its design brings the evolution of the locomotive full circle from the universal American Standard, to highly specialized designs and wheel arrangements, back to a general-purpose locomotive. It was limited to mainline applications on most carriers because of its high axle loadings.

The First 4-8-4s

In 1926, Northern Pacific worked with Alco to develop the 4-8-4 to supplant Pacific types on crack (priority) passenger trains. Alco delivered the first 4-8-4s to NP in early 1927, and designated them Class A. Prior to these locomotives, NP had resisted using an eight-coupled locomotive in passenger service, and its 4-8-4 design was essentially an adaptation of the 4-8-2 Mountain type, capable of burning low-energy Rosebud coal. This coal was available from company mines in Montana and cost roughly

Santa Fe's first 4-8-4, number 3751, was restored to service in 1991. On December 28, 1991, it leads a passenger excursion over California's Tehachapi Mountains. The 3751 and a pair of Santa Fe's colorfully painted FP45 diesels are seen descending the Tehachapi grade near old Allard, between Bealville and Caliente, California. This line was built, owned, and operated by the Southern Pacific, but was shared with Santa Fe. *Jim Speaker, courtesy of Brian Jennison*

70 percent less than high-energy Eastern coal, making it an especially attractive fuel for locomotives despite its low-energy content. Rosebud coal's higher ash content required a significantly larger and heavier firebox than the conventional 4-8-2 type used to ensure effective burning. This mandated a four-wheel trailing truck to keep axle loadings within acceptable limits. NP's 4-8-4s used a 115-square-foot firebox grate, 52.5 percent larger than New York Central's L-2a 4-8-2s built in 1926. The NP firebox was also larger than most subsequent 4-8-4 designs, many of which were significantly more powerful locomotives. If NP was looking only for a high-capacity firebox, why didn't it adopt a 2-8-4 Berkshire type similar to those used on the Boston & Albany? The answer is simple: speed. NP wanted to run its passenger trains fast, and the Berkshire type was not well suited to that type of service.

Canadian National 6218 is a Class U-2-g 4-8-4 that was built by the Montreal Locomotive Works, Alco's Canadian affiliate, in September 1942. It was a typical example of CN's later 4-8-4s featuring 73-inch drivers, which made it ideal for both passenger and freight work. It is seen hauling an excursion in Quebec in October 1964. *Richard Jay Solomon*

Canadian National 6218 hauls an excursion at Islington Avenue, Etobicoke, Toronto, Ontario, on March 21, 1971. Canadian National operated its 4-8-4s in both freight and passenger service. CN 6218 is now preserved at Fort Erie, Ontario, across the border from Buffalo, New York. *Fred Matthews*

NP's 4-8-4s featured 73-inch drivers—a standard size on many Mountain types of the period and ideal for fast passenger work. The locomotives weighed 426,000 pounds, featuring just 65,000 pounds per axle—roughly the same amount as NP's Pacifics and the maximum the railroad was designed for at that time. NP's pioneering 4-8-4s were proportionally different from most subsequent 4-8-4s in several noticeable respects. They used a smaller boiler and featured an elongated smokebox situated at the front of the locomotive beneath the stack. They had unusually large ash pans (located beneath the firebox) to accommodate the high ash content of Rosebud coal.

The new type met with success on NP, which had suffered from a variety of difficulties with its modern Pacifics. While these 4-8-4s did not establish

Canadian National operated more 4-8-4s than any other railroad in North America. Its 4-8-4s were lightweights compared to most operated in the United States. No. 6218 weighed just 399,000 pounds, 110,000 pounds less than Santa Fe's big 4-8-4s of the same period. CN 6218 leads an excursion across a large trestle in Quebec in October 1964. *Richard Jay Solomon*

any new power records—according to Alfred Bruce they developed only 61,500 pounds tractive effort, about the same as many conventional midsized 4-8-2s of the period—they were capable of handling a heavy passenger train over a 1 percent grade, allowing NP to eliminate passenger helpers and double-heading on all but its steepest grades. This greatly reduced costs. NP was very satisfied with the type and placed several repeat orders for 4-8-4s. These later locomotives featured larger boilers, slightly larger cylinders, and 77-inch driving wheels. Except for the single Alco-built 4-8-4 that NP bought secondhand from Timken (this was the famous *Four Aces* roller-bearing demonstrator), NP's later 4-8-4s were all Baldwin products and also featured enormous fireboxes. The success of the large firebox and four-wheeled trailing truck led NP

to investigate the 2-8-8-4 type with some success (see chapter 5).

Within a year of NP's debut of the 4-8-4 Northern, three other North American railroads adopted the type. Shortly after NP received its passenger locomotives, Alco delivered 4-8-4s featuring 77-inch drivers to the Lackawanna, intended for passenger service. Baldwin built a fleet of exceptional machines with 73-inch drivers for Santa Fe (see below). Canadian National embraced the 4-8-4 with great enthusiasm, starting with an order for 40 and ultimately featuring the largest roster of 4-8-4s in North America, some 203 locomotives, including those of its Grand Trunk Western subsidiary. Canadian National's 4-8-4s were handsome, powerful dual-service machines, but relatively lightweight

While some modern steam locomotives were preserved, many types were not. All of Lackawanna's famous 4-8-4 Poconos were scrapped, so when Pennsylvania-based Steamtown wanted to represent a Pocono in a promotional film, it borrowed a Milwaukee Road 261 and dressed it up as Lackawanna 1661. On October 11, 1994, the disguised locomotive rolls through Waukesha, Wisconsin, on the Wisconsin Central. *Brian Solomon*

compared to those used on most American railways. CN's first order weighed only 378,000 pounds and its axle loadings were less than 58,000 pounds. Later 4-8-4s, such as U-2h 4-8-4s built by Montreal in 1943, were only marginally heavier, weighing just 400,300 pounds and placing only 246,100 pounds on the drivers (axle loading of 61,525 pounds). Light axle loading gave CN great flexibility with its 4-8-4 fleet and it operated them all across its vast North American railway network.

More 4-8-4s

While the 4-8-4 was not built in numbers as vast as the popular presuperpower types, by the late 1920s, the 4-8-4 had emerged as the preferred locomotive on American railroads and more 4-8-4s were ordered than any other superpowered design. Approximately 1,000 4-8-4s were built for service in North America. Of these, many were exceptional locomotives. The combination of the large boiler

The Reading was an anthracite coal–hauling line in eastern Pennsylvania and one of the last railroads to adopt the 4-8-4. After Reading discontinued its regular steam operations, it assigned three Class T-1 4-8-4s to excursion service. One of these locomotives leads a "Reading Ramble" in eastern Pennsylvania on a pleasant day in October 1964. *Richard Jay Solomon*

A pair of Reading T-1s, led by No. 2100, haul a well-patronized "Reading Ramble" excursion in eastern Pennsylvania on a crisp October day in 1963. Between 1945 and 1947, Reading constructed 30 4-8-4s using boilers from old 2-8-0 Consolidations. The T-1 4-8-4s were intended for freight service, but three of them operated in passenger excursion service after Reading dieselized its freight operations. *Richard Jay Solomon*

capacity and modern accessories was powerful, and the well-balanced design with large drivers gave them a good steady ride, so 4-8-4s were popular with operating departments and engineers alike. They worked a variety of premier passenger and freight duties, often assigned to relatively long runs. The Wabash, a midwestern bridge line, owned 18 4-8-4s with 70-inch drivers, and used them on fast freights. They typically handled the 272-mile run between Decatur, Illinois, and Montpelier, Ohio. The Lehigh Valley operated 37 4-8-4 Wyomings and routinely assigned them to fast freights that covered the full length of its mainline, a distance of 450 miles from Jersey City to Buffalo. But where the 4-8-4 really made a difference was west of the Mississippi. Western railroads made the longest runs, and pioneer 4-8-4 operator Northern Pacific claimed the prize for the longest regular runs with a coal-burning locomotive, a distance

of just over 1,000 miles. However, Santa Fe's oil-burning 4-8-4s operated halfway across the nation, running from Kansas City, Missouri, to Los Angeles, more than 1,760 miles.

The Reading, an anthracite coal hauler serving eastern Pennsylvania, adopted the 4-8-4 for freight service much later than its coal hauling neighbors,

Next Page
In 1947, Santa Fe 2925 departs Belen, New Mexico, with the *Scout*. Santa Fe's 2900 Class 4-8-4s were among the most impressive locomotives ever built. They were regularly assigned runs more than 1,700 miles long, produced 66,000 pounds tractive effort, and could easily reach 100 miles per hour with a heavy passenger train. To keep smoke from blowing into the cab, these locomotives were equipped with an adjustable stack extension, seen fully extended in this photo. *Otto Perry, Denver Public Library Western History Department*

the Lackawanna and the Lehigh Valley. Between 1945 and 1947, Reading built 30 4-8-4s at its Reading, Pennsylvania, shops using boiler components from retired 2-8-0 Consolidations. Classed T-1 and assigned freight duties, they were midsized Northerns, featuring 27x32-inch cylinders, 70-inch drivers, 94.5-square-foot firebox grates, and operated at 240-psi boiler pressure. They weighed 441,300 pounds, with 278,200 pounds on drivers, and delivered 68,000 pounds tractive effort, plus an additional 11,100 pounds with a trailing truck booster. Three of Reading's T-1s survived the diesel onslaught in the late 1950s and enjoyed extended careers in excursion service.

The Norfolk & Western J-class 4-8-4 is considered one of the finest steam locomotives ever built. On April 18, 1958, an N&W J leads the westbound *Cavalier* downgrade at Maybeury, West Virginia. *George Diamond*

Western Maryland, another coal-hauling line that also interchanged a fair quantity of freight with Reading as part of the so-called Alphabet Route, bought the very last 4-8-4s designed for freight service. Western Maryland's 12 4-8-4s were known as Potomacs and were built by Baldwin in 1947.

Santa Fe was one of the first railroads to adopt the 4-8-4, and its very first was No. 3751, built by Baldwin in 1927. This historic locomotive was preserved, and in the early 1990s, it was restored to service. On December 30, 1991, it leads an excursion through Azusa, California. *James A. Speaker*

Southern Pacific GS-4 4449 at Brock, California, on April 28, 1991. *Brian Solomon*

The Finest 4-8-4s

The 4-8-4 Northern type was one of the best wheel arrangements ever used on an American locomotive and while there are numerous examples of superlative performance, a few stand out above the rest and are remembered as some of the finest locomotives ever built. For years locomotive chronologers have discussed and debated which engines gave superior performance, but this text will simply illustrate some of the most impressive examples of 4-8-4s. Since each locomotive was designed for operation on different lines, it is difficult to decide which one was the top performer.

Santa Fe

Santa Fe's pioneer interest in the 4-8-4 type ultimately resulted in one of the most successful fleets. Between 1935 and 1937, Santa Fe upgraded the original 1927 4-8-4s, equipping them with 80-inch drivers and roller bearings, converting them from coal to oil operation, and raising working boiler pressure from 210 psi to 230 psi. However, Santa Fe's best

Southern Pacific 4449, a streamlined 4-8-4 built by Lima in 1941, is undoubtedly one of the most famous locomotives in America. Recently, it was featured in a painting by artist Ted Rose on a 33-cent stamp issued by the United States Postal Service. Here it is seen climbing past Worden, Oregon, on April 28, 1991, on its way to Railfair 1991 in Sacramento, California. *Brian Solomon*

Milwaukee Road was famous for its high-speed streamlined 4-4-2 Atlantics and 4-6-4s, but it also streamlined some older power. It rebuilt two of its F5 Pacifics with Otto Kuhler-designed shrouds for service on the Sioux Falls, South Dakota, section of the *Midwest Hiawatha*. Streamlined Pacific No. 801 is seen at Sioux City, Iowa, in the 1940s. *Leon Onofri collection, courtesy of Robert W. Jones*

Northerns were those built by Baldwin between 1938 and 1944. There were three separate orders, each considered a different class and identified by the number of the first locomotive in the group (a standard Santa Fe practice). Eleven 3765s were delivered in 1938, followed by 10 3776s in 1941, and 30 2900s in 1943 and 1944. All employed 80-inch drivers, 28x32-inch cylinders, operated at 300-psi boiler pressure, and were intended for fast passenger service. The 2900s and 3776s were extremely powerful machines. The 3776s worked with a 70 percent cut-off, delivering 66,000 pounds tractive effort and producing more than 5,000 horsepower. The 2900/3776s operated continuously at 90 miles per hour and have been known to operate at more than 100 miles per hour, making them some of the largest

Southern Pacific's classy GS-4 and GS-5 Northerns can be distinguished from other models by their dual headlight arrangement. These locomotives featured both conventional and oscillating headlights. Later, oscillating headlights were standard equipment on Southern Pacific diesels. *Brian Solomon*

and fastest steam locomotives ever built. Santa Fe's line to California has plenty of tangent track, ideal for swift running. There are many places in the Mojave desert (in Southern California, across Arizona, and in the New Mexico desert) where a 4-8-4 could clip along at maximum speed for mile after mile without needing to slow for a curve. Nevertheless, Santa Fe's grade profile was hardly level, and there was a great deal of climbing up and down on the railroad between Kansas City and California. While the 4-8-4s were capable of fast speed, they were

Southern Pacific GS-4 4449 leads an eastbound excursion along the shore of San Pablo Bay at Pinole, California, in May 1991. In Southern Pacific's classification system, 4-8-4s were classified as GS, initials that stood for "General Service" or "Golden State." While these handsome, powerful locomotives were often used to haul SP's finest passenger trains, they also worked freight assignments. *Brian Solomon*

also designed to operate on heavy grades. Even the best locomotives have their limits, however. Santa Fe's famous Raton and Glorieta Passes in New Mexico and its Cajon Pass in California all feature stretches of 3 percent grade, making them some of the steepest sections of mainline track in the United States. For these especially tough climbs, most trains, even those behind the 4-8-4s, required extra help. Trains typically stopped at the base of these grades for additional "helper" locomotives to be tied on.

On a more level track, a single 4-8-4 could haul 15 traditional heavyweight passenger cars, and up to 17 modern streamlined cars at maximum speed. What could be more impressive than watching one of these great locomotives race along at 90 miles per hour? One of these powerful, precision machines charging across the sunny high plateaus of northern New Mexico, covering a mile and a half of track every 60 seconds, was once a daily event. This fast operation was not an anomaly but routine, safe transportation. To allow for trains to follow fairly closely a high speed, without the risk of collision, Santa Fe— like many railroads- installed a protective signaling system. Silent sentinels—semaphores—would mark the passing 4-8-4 and train by dropping from the vertical position to horizontal, thus protecting the rear of the train against a following train, until it had reached the next 'block' several miles away, when the semaphore would rise to a "caution" indication. In the days of peak passenger travel, a popular train such as the *Chief* might run in several sections, each section being an individual train set with its own locomotive. Good signalling was, and still is, as important as powerful locomotives in the operation of fast trains.

Mighty Limas

Southern Pacific's Lima-built 4-8-4 streamliners are some of the most recognizable locomotives in the United States, and certainly among the most

Southern Pacific's last new 4-8-4s were 10 GS-6s built by Lima in 1943. These were built to comply with War Production Board restrictions and were less impressive than SP's earlier GS-4 and GS-5 4-8-4s. They used smaller drivers, and did not feature the elaborate *Daylight* coloring as SP's earlier Lima 4-8-4s. *Fred Matthews*

Southern Pacific 4449 races up the Sacramento River Canyon toward Dunsmuir, California. *Brian Solomon*

Chesapeake & Ohio 614 leads an excursion at Salisbury Mills, New York, on the former Erie Railroad in June 1997. C&O's five J-3-A 4-8-4s, Nos. 610 to 614, were built by Lima in 1948, making them some of the last 4-8-4s built in the United States. *Brian Solomon*

impressive 4-8-4s ever constructed. They were not SP's first Northerns: the railroad bought conventional-looking SP-class GS-1 Baldwins in 1930. The Lima streamlined 4-8-4s were intended for service on SP's flashy new *Daylight*. Initially SP ordered six Lima 4-8-4s in 1936—class GS-2s intended for fast passenger service. They featured 27x30-inch cylinders, 73.5-inch drivers, weighed 448,400 pounds, and produced 75,950 pounds tractive effort with booster. The *Daylight* would regularly operate at 80 miles per hour, and these locomotives were capable of at least 90 miles per hour. Southern Pacific followed up by ordering 15 more 4-8-4s from Lima in 1937. These were bigger, heavier, and even more impressive. Designated as class GS-3, they featured 26x32-inch cylinders, 80-inch drivers, operated at 280-psi boiler pressure (higher than the 250 psi on SP's earlier Northerns), weighed 460,000 pounds, and delivered 76,650 pounds tractive effort (with booster).

The zenith of the SP's Northerns—the definitive *Daylight* locomotive—is the GS-4. In 1941, SP received 28 GS-4s from Lima, numbers 4430 to 4457. Like the GS-3s, these featured 26x32-inch cylinders and 80-inch drivers. However, they were 15,000 pounds heavier, operated at 300-psi boiler pressure, and produced 78,650 pounds tractive effort (with booster). They looked more impressive too, and featured a distinctive dual headlight arrangement that included a highlight and oscillating headlight. In 1942, SP took delivery of two GS-5s, which were nearly identical to the GS-4s except they were slightly heavier and equipped with roller bearings.

During WWII, SP acquired its last new passenger locomotives: 10 GS-6s, built by Lima. SP needed to adhere to wartime restrictions, and as a result,

built less impressive machines. While still semi-streamlined, these locomotives had a more conservative appearance and dressed in black paint instead of the bright *Daylight* colors. During the war, Western Pacific also received locomotives built to the GS-6 specifications.

Southern Pacific's magnificent 4-8-4 streamliners were largely assigned to passenger work, hauling SP's most famous passenger trains such as the *Daylight, Lark,* and *Sunset Limited,* but they also were assigned to freight traffic from time to time. In their later days, the once colorful *Daylight* 4-8-4s were stripped of much of their shrouding, painted black, and regularly assigned to secondary passenger runs and freights. Two late-era SP 4-8-4s were preserved: GS-6, a locomotive that hauled one of SP's last steam trains, is at the Museum of Transport in St. Louis, and GS-4 4449 was displayed at Oaks Park in Portland, Oregon, until the 1970s when it was restored to service for the American Freedom train. In 1981, it was restored to its original appearance and still operates in occasional excursion service today.

In 1948, Lima built 5 exceptional 4-8-4s for steam holdout Chesapeake & Ohio, giving the railroad a total of 12 of the type (two earlier orders of five and two locomotives each were built by Lima in 1935 and 1941 respectively). Known as Greenbriers—named for the Greenbrier River in the heart of C&O's territory—these locomotives were designed for heavy passenger service. While they were not the heaviest, fastest, most powerful, or best-looking 4-8-4s, they were superlative machines and among the last of the type constructed, so they should be mentioned in any list of the best 4-8-4s ever built. They featured 72-inch driving wheels, 27.5x30-inch cylinders, 100.3-square-foot grate, operated at 255-psi boiler pressure, weighed 479,400 pounds with 282,400 pounds on drivers, and delivered 68,300 pounds tractive effort, plus 12,400 pounds with booster (total tractive effort 78,850 pounds). This final order of C&O Greenbriers

was distinguished from the earlier ones by the use of modern equipment associated with the modern steam-power designs, including roller bearings on all axles, siderods, aluminum cabs and boiler jacketing, and other late-era equipment and accessories.

The Greenbriers could easily handle a 14-car train of traditional heavyweight cars up C&O's famous Allegheny grade and, in their earlier years, they were primarily passenger locomotives. In the mid-1950s, after diesels had assumed most passenger runs, C&O found work for its 4-8-4s hauling fast freight.

Union Pacific 800s

Union Pacific was not among the first users of the 4-8-4 and was content to employ 4-8-2 Mountains and other types on its primary passenger runs a decade after Northern Pacific and Santa Fe had introduced the type for passenger service. It is also notable that Union Pacific chose to develop the 4-8-4 several years after it had inaugurated some of the nation's first diesel-powered passenger trains. In February 1934, UP debuted America's first internal combustion streamlined passenger train: a Pullman-built three-car articulated machine powered by a Winton distillate-burning engine, which was originally known as the *Streamliner.* This train toured the United States and is considered, along with Burlington's *Zephyr,* one of the predecessors to Electro-Motive's E-unit, the locomotive that ultimately bumped most modern steam locomotives from premier passenger work. The success of the *Streamliner* led Union Pacific to invest in a fleet of diesel-powered streamlined trains. By the time UP's first 4-8-4s were being drawn up, the diesel had already gained a significant foothold in Union Pacific's motive power fleet. UP felt that it required more powerful steam locomotives to accommodate its heavy, high-speed passenger trains. Its first 20 4-8-4s, numbered 800 to 819, were built by Alco in 1937. They embodied many elements of modern locomotive design, including one-piece cast integral bed frames, Timken roller bearings on all axles—a first for Union Pacific—and valve gears equipped with needle bearings. The locomotives employed 77-inch Boxpok drivers and 24.5x32-inch cylinders.

UP was very pleased with their 4-8-4s, and despite a growing interest in diesels, refined and improved the Northern type and placed two additional orders for 4-8-4s with Alco, which were delivered in 1939 and 1944. These later machines are especially impressive, featuring 80-inch drivers, 25x32-inch cylinders, a 100.2-square-foot grate, and operated at 300-psi boiler pressure. They weighed 478,640 pounds with 270,300 pounds on drivers. (The last 10 locomotives, numbered 835 to 844, were slightly heavier, weighing 490,700 pounds, but the weight on the drivers remained the same.)

The 800s were fast, powerful engines designed to operate at a sustained 90 miles per hour with a

Union Pacific 4-8-4 No. 844 leads a short freight westward at Grand Island, Nebraska. *Brian Solomon*

1,000-ton passenger train. They were counterbalanced for 110 miles per hour and are reported to have exceeded 100 miles per hour on occasion. It is said that their top speed is limited only by the engineer's nerve. Equally impressive was their exceptional 93 percent availability for service, a figure comparable with diesels, and a vast improvement over UP's 4-8-2s. The 800s regularly worked approximately 15,000 miles a month.

UP's 4-8-4 No. 844 has earned special significance. The last in the class, the 844 escaped retirement, has operated nearly every year since it rolled out of Alco in 1944, and has remained serviceable through the 1990s. It is one of the few steam locomotives still owned and operated by its original owner, a rare distinction for an American engine.

Niagaras

New York Central's Niagara was unquestionably one of the finest steam locomotives ever conceived. It was the work of Central's locomotive genius, Paul Kiefer, and represents the culmination of more than 120 years of steam locomotive development. The 4-8-4 type was reaching its 18th birthday before New York Central developed it for regular use, making it among the very last railroads to embrace this popular locomotive design. It wasn't Central's first 4-8-4. In 1930, the railroad had experimented with a unique high-pressure, three-cylinder compound in a 4-8-4 arrangement, but this locomotive had virtually no influence on its Niagara designs, which were an expansion of its 4-8-2 Mohawk type and incorporated technological refinements used on its 4-6-4 Hudsons (see chapter 3).

One of the most interesting aspects of New York Central's decision to develop the Niagara was its timing. By the end of World War II, most American railroads looked toward dieselization and few new steam locomotives were being developed. Most of the designs built during the war were adaptations of existing locomotives. Furthermore, many were ordered only because the War Production Board denied railways the diesels they desired. However, this was not the case with New York Central. It was one of a few remaining carriers that still believed in traditional reciprocating steam locomotives.

Paul Kiefer believed that a steam locomotive could offer a competitive motive power solution and designed a prototype super 4-8-4 intended for both high-speed passenger service and fast freight service. He was faced with making the new locomotive conform to New York Central's unusually tight clearances. A New York Central locomotive could be no wider than 10 feet 5 inches and no taller than 15 feet 3 inches. This height requirement was especially constraining and posed serious restrictions on the ultimate size of the locomotive boiler. Kiefer overcame these restrictions and developed an especially modern locomotive.

The prototype Niagara, No. 6000—New York Central class S-1a—was constructed by Alco in August 1945, just as World War II was coming to a close. It was intended to expand on the potential of the L-4, 4-8-2 Mohawk, which Kiefer had refined a few years earlier. The S-1a's enormous boiler was built to the limits of New York Central clearances. In order to allow for more boiler space, Kiefer dispensed with the conventional steam dome and employed an internal dry pipe for steam collection instead. Boiler pressure was set at 290 psi, and the firebox had a 101-square-foot grate—24.7 square feet

Mainline freight with steam power in the 1980s? Union Pacific 844 has made numerous appearances since the end of regular steam operations as a passenger excursion locomotive, and on rare occasion, the locomotive has also been used to haul freight. In September 1989, Union Pacific 844 hauls a westbound freight across the Burlington Northern crossing at Grand Island, Nebraska. *Brian Solomon*

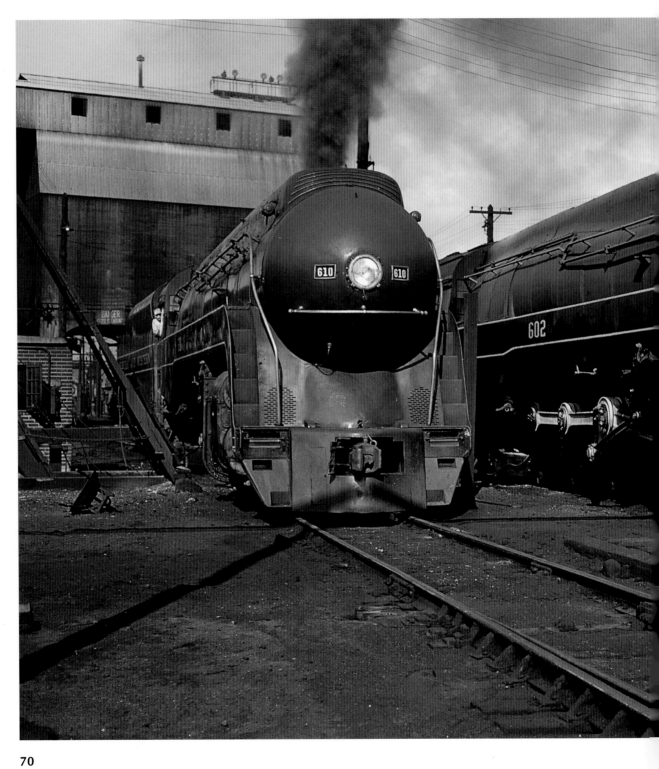

larger than his L-4 design. Its cylinders were 25x32 inches, and it used Baker valve gear. Like other modern New York Central locomotives, including its famous J-3a Hudsons and some of its late-era Mohawks, the Niagara employed lightweight alloy steel reciprocating parts. Main rods were made from manganese-vanadium steel. To keep axle weight down, they were constructed of carbon-vanadium steel. Weight was further reduced by employing aluminum in cab construction, on the running boards, on the "elephant ear" smoke lifters, and for other parts that did not require great strength, making the Niagara one of the few American steam locomotives to use the lightweight metal. Like other modern 4-8-4s it used a cast-steel, integral bed frame, and all axles and reciprocating parts were equipped with Timken roller bearings.

The locomotive weighed 471,000 pounds, making it noticeably lighter than many other late-era 4-8-4s. (Santa Fe's 2900 weighed more than 500,000 pounds). Yet, it placed 275,000 pounds on the driving wheels, giving it relatively high axle loadings for a New York Central locomotive. Its tender used a centipede wheel arrangement similar to that used by Union Pacific. Initially the locomotive was equipped with 75-inch drivers, but these were soon replaced with 79-inch drivers. The Niagara proved extremely powerful. It produced 62,400 maximum tractive effort and developed 6,600 maximum cylinder horsepower at 77 miles per hour (maximum drawbar horsepower was 5,050 at 63 miles per hour). It could haul an 18-car passenger train at a sustained 80 miles

A pair of Norfolk & Western Js rest at Shaffers Crossing in Roanoke, Virginia. The N&W was the last railroad to acquire new steam power and the last to acquire streamlined steam. N&W was unusual because it built its own steam power. It had a total of 14 streamlined 4-8-4s but also operated very similar-looking 4-8-2s. It built its last three Js in 1950, nine years after the first five.
Richard Jay Solomon

per hour without straining. New York Central had intended its output to match Electro-Motive's new E-units, and there was little doubt that it passed this test.

New York Central seemed pleased with the prototype's performance and ordered another 26 Niagaras in 1945 and 1946. Twenty-five were class S-1bs and in most respects resembled the prototype. They operated only at 275 psi, which resulted in maximum tractive effort of 61,570 pounds, slightly less that the S-1a prototype. The S-1bs were all equipped with 79-inch drivers and Baker valve gear. The last locomotive, class S-2a, was different from the rest and featured Franklin rotary-cam actuated poppet valves instead of the more conventional piston valves and valve gear.

The Niagaras demonstrated extraordinary service and performance. They averaged more than 850 miles per day, and regularly ran more than 25,000 miles a month, sometimes reaching as many as 27,000 miles per month. They proved to be extremely reliable and provided more than adequate power for their intended service. However, while the mighty Niagaras equaled diesel performance, they did so at greater cost. Despite their superlative performance, they were quickly bumped by diesels from choice runs, and within a decade of their construction they were gone.

Norfolk & Western Js

Coal-hauling Norfolk & Western is legendary for holding onto steam power longer than any other major line in the United States. In the mid-1950s, several years after some lines had completely converted to diesel power and most American railroads were contemplating total dieselization

In 1937 and 1938, Milwaukee bought 30 Baldwin 4-8-4s, Class S-2, for freight service. By the mid-1950s, steam operations were coming to an end on the Milwaukee Road and in October 1956, No. 204 was the last S-2 4-8-4 to roll into Milwaukee, Wisconsin. *Russ Porter*

within a few more years, N&W stood out as the sole remaining holdout for big-time steam operations. Norfolk & Western is a special case because not only did it hold onto steam unusually late, it also constructed most of its own locomotives, which stand out as some of the most refined designs ever built. Among the most impressive products of N&W's Roanoke shop were 14 Northern types, known as Class Js. They were spectacular machines that defied convention and set performance and reliability records. The first five Js were built during 1941 and 1942, with N&W's distinctive streamlined shrouds and featuring 27x32-inch cylinders, 70-inch drivers, a 107.7-square-foot firebox grate, and a huge boiler set for 275 psi operation. These locomotives delivered 73,300 pounds tractive effort. (N&W later increased the boiler pressure to 300 psi, thus increasing tractive effort to 80,000 pounds.) The J class exhibited all of the trappings of the modern locomotive, featuring roller bearings on all axles and reciprocating parts, one-piece cast-steel frame, mechanical lubrication, and lightweight alloy-steel rods (Timken's lightweight tandem main rods). The second order of Js were built in 1942 and 1943, and, like many high-performance locomotives, suffered from War Production Board restrictions. For a short time, these locomotives were known as J-1s. They were delivered without the decorative streamlined shrouding and came with bulky heavy rods made of conventional instead of lightweight steel. Following the war, N&W sent these Js to the shop for modification. When they emerged, they were practically indistinguishable from the original order. In 1950, N&W made history by building the last three 4-8-4s, as well as the last new passenger steam locomotives in the United States. Like the other Js, these sported streamlined shrouds, years after some lines, such as the New York Central (see chapter 4), had removed streamlined elements from their passenger engines.

N&W had its own ideas on motive power and did not follow common trends regarding development or application. So where the national trend for passenger 4-8-4s was toward larger driving wheels—typically in the 77- to 80-inch range—the J's wheels at just 70 inches were some of the smallest ever used for a passenger design. Yet the Js were not slow locomotives. In fact, they were some of the fastest 4-8-4s ever designed. In a test run, a J achieved 110 miles per hour hauling a 15-car train weighing 1,025 tons! N&W compensated for the smaller driving wheels by using precision counterbalancing. Running maintenance was another N&W forte. It kept its locomotives in excellent shape and used modern facilities it called "lubritoriums" to speed routine lubrication procedures. The results were evident in their exceptionally smooth-running machines.

The Js were notable for their excellent service. They routinely operated 15,000 miles per month, often running more than 500 miles per day. This performance was among the best in the nation for steam. It even exceeded that offered by diesel-electrics on many routes--a fact that astounded some locomotive authorities because of the nature of N&W's relatively short, heavily graded mainline. Unlike Santa Fe, Union Pacific, and New York Central, N&W was not running vast distances on high-speed mainlines. It's no wonder N&W held off diesels longer than anyone else.

Yet keeping those streamlined steam locomotives moving, and moving fast, was a matter of company pride. Where N&W's articulated monsters were earning their keep hauling coal from West Virginia mines, the Js were operating at a loss. Even with their exemplary performance statistics, N&W's passenger trains, like most others in the United States at that time, did not break even. Shortly after N&W steam vanished, many of its passenger trains vanished as well.

Articulated Locomotives

Its boiler delivers 7,000 horsepower, it has a cruising speed of eighty miles an hour, and consumes twelve tons of coal and 15,000 gallons of water every sixty minutes.

—Lucius Beebe
describing a Union Pacific Big Boy in *Trains in Transition*

Late-era steam development produced gargantuan, powerful machines unlike anything ever seen before or since. Locomotives in America were the biggest, heaviest, and most powerful in the world. The Yellowstone, the Big Boy, and the Allegheny were

Union Pacific 4-6-6-4 Challenger 3985 leads an excursion over the former Western Pacific at Altamont Pass near Livermore, California, in July 1992. The Challenger was designed for high-speed service. The type proved to be versatile and was used by a variety of railroads in the East and West. *Brian Solomon*

75

Norfolk & Western Y6 2-8-8-2 No. 2129 drifts downgrade at Blue Ridge, Virginia, after working as a pusher on the end of a heavy freight. A compound locomotive is easily identified by its enormous low-pressure front cylinders. By 1958, N&W was one of the last railroads operating big steam, and its compounds were a technological anomaly; most American railroads abandoned compound steam designs in the 1920s. *Richard Jay Solomon*

all known at various times as the world's largest locomotive. These monstrous machines, the biggest of the big, were simple articulated types that used two sets of running gear under the control of a single throttle below one giant boiler. The Mallet, another enormously powerful locomotive, used a compound arrangement that was not conducive to faster operations on most railroads. The railroads that used these great machines had a long legacy of applying the largest locomotives to haul the longest and heaviest trains possible. The largest simple articulateds were built for heavy freight service. Yet, simple articulated locomotives were also developed for fairly fast running, and different types emerged to

satisfy a variety of heavy railroad applications, including fast freight and passenger services. There is no denying that these highly refined supersteam locomotives are some of the most impressive machines ever built.

Mallets

The articulated locomotive was introduced to American railroading in 1904 at the St. Louis Exposition. Baltimore & Ohio's famous Mallet Compound, commonly known as "Old Maud," used an 0-6-6-0 wheel arrangement. The Mallet Compound was initially used as a rear-end helper locomotive in heavy freight service but was adapted to mainline service by

Duluth, Missabe & Iron Range operated a fleet of 18 Yellowstones built by Baldwin between 1943 and 1945. They were massive machines designed to haul heavy iron ore trains from the Minnesota Iron Range to docks on Lake Superior. DM&IR 231 is under steam at the Proctor, Minnesota, engine facility in 1959. *Russ Porter*

Baldwin for the Great Northern in 1906. It quickly became a popular type for heavy, slow-speed freight service and thousands were built, using a variety of wheel arrangements, for heavy service all around the United States. Mallets were especially popular on coal-hauling lines and steep mountain grades where exceptional power was needed and speed was not an issue. While Mallets were extremely powerful and capable of delivering enormous tractive effort (Virginian's 2-10-10-2 Mallets produced 176,600 pounds starting tractive effort, the most of any reciprocating steam locomotive ever built), they were limited to slow speeds by small wheels, unstable front sections, and problems with back pressure in the low-pressure cylinders. So while they were ideal for heavy drag

work, most Mallets were not practical for moving trains much faster than about 20 miles per hour. As a result, Mallets fell out of favor in the 1920s when newer, more efficient, and faster types were developed to meet the railroads' desire to operate faster freights.

One of these successful new locomotive designs was an adaptation of the Mallet: the simple articulated used two sets of high-pressure cylinders instead of the high-pressure and low-pressure system used on compound locomotives. The simple articulated had been first tried as early as 1912 by the Pennsylvania Railroad, which found it unsuccessful and did not follow up with further development.

In 1924, the Chesapeake & Ohio was the first railroad to employ a fleet of simple articulateds in

Duluth, Missabe & Iron Range 2-8-8-4 Yellowstone 222 leads an excursion train at Biwabic, Minnesota, in July 1958. These powerful machines spent most of their careers working in demanding ore train service. They survived longer than most big steam, working through the 1950s, and three are preserved today. *Russ Porter*

regular freight service. Its 2-8-8-2 simples had ample boiler capacity to maintain significantly higher speeds than the typical Mallet Compound of the period. A year later, Great Northern bought a fleet of similar locomotives from Baldwin. By the late 1920s, a number of railroads had fleets of simple articulateds, and some were modifying older Mallets to simple operation.

The Yellowstone

The development of the four-wheel, load-bearing, trailing truck was first used by Northern Pacific in 1928 on an enormous experimental simple articulated with a 2-8-8-4 wheel arrangement. This locomotive was designed to solve an unusual operating problem. NP's Yellowstone district between Glendive, Montana, and Mandan, North Dakota, features a rugged "sawtooth" profile (a series of short pronounced grades with multiple summits that resemble a saw blade on a grade profile map). This district was particularly difficult to operate because unlike NP's longer, steeper grades farther west, it was not conducive to helper operations. As a result, NP was forced to run shorter, more frequent trains, which dramatically increased its costs. The 2-8-8-4 was designed to haul significantly heavier trains and simplify operations east of Glendive. The reason this giant was so unusual was that it needed to burn NP's low-grade Rosebud coal, which required a phenomenally large firebox—the largest on any locomotive ever built. The firebox was 22 feet long and 9 feet wide and had a tapered top that ranged from 8 feet high to slightly more than 6 feet. The 182-square-foot firebox grate was by far the largest ever used. Its exceptional weight necessitated

During World War II, the Baltimore & Ohio wanted Electro-Motive diesels. When B&O was denied them by the War Production Board, it turned to Baldwin for 2-8-8-4 Yellowstones instead. Two of B&O's EM1 Yellowstones are seen at Painesville, Ohio, on August 8, 1956. *George Diamond*

the use of the four-wheel trailing truck that NP had first used a couple of years earlier on the first 4-8-4 (see chapter 4), which, like the 2-8-8-4, was also designed to burn Rosebud coal.

When it was built, Northern Pacific's 2-8-8-4 was indisputably the largest locomotive in the world—a title it held for more than a decade—and among the most powerful ever designed. The prototype weighed 717,000 pounds, measured 66 feet, 8 inches long (nearly 112 feet including tender), and delivered 140,000 pounds tractive effort, plus 13,400 pounds with booster. It was named for the Yellowstone Division, which followed the Yellowstone River in eastern

Engineer Ed App oils the tender to Yellowstone 2-8-8-4 No. 228 prior to its departure from Proctor Yard (Minnesota) on May 26, 1959. The Duluth, Missabe & Iron Range was one of the last railroads in the Midwest to regularly operate big steam. Its Yellowstones were very similar to Northern Pacific's originals. *William D. Middleton*

Montana. While NP initially encountered some problems with the Alco-built 2-8-8-4 prototype, it felt the locomotive would fulfill the service for which it was designed and ordered 11 more. Oddly these locomotives were not built by Alco, but by its primary competitor, Baldwin. NP probably chose Baldwin because it built the 2-8-8-4 at a better price, despite Alco's work on the prototype. Initially, all the Yellowstones worked the territory for which they had been built, but in later years several locomotives were transferred west and worked as helpers on Bozeman Pass out of Livingston, Montana.

More Yellowstones

While the 2-8-8-4 wheel arrangement was never popular, several other lines purchased Yellowstones for heavy service. Southern Pacific, which was famous for its cab-forward articulateds (see below), ordered 10 conventionally oriented 2-8-8-4s, class AC-9, from Lima in 1938. (AC in SP locomotive lexicon stood for

Union Pacific 3985 is an extremely impressive piece of machinery and the largest working steam locomotive in the world today. Larger locomotives are preserved, but none of them have operated in decades. UP's Challenger pauses at Baker City, Oregon, in June 1993 after running over the Blue Mountains in northeastern Oregon. *Brian Solomon*

articulated consolidation, as a 2-8-8-4 was essentially two 2-8-0 Consolidations under a single boiler.) These handsomely proportioned machines shared a semi-streamlined look with SP's famous Lima-built

Baltimore & Ohio originally assigned its 2-8-8-4 EM1s to its rugged West End line, between Grafton, West Virginia, and Cumberland, Maryland. In later years, they mostly worked coal lines in Ohio and Pennsylvania. B&O EM1 7611 leads an empty hopper train from Painesville, Ohio, to New Castle, Pennsylvania, on Aug. 8, 1956. *George Diamond*

Northerns. ACs were built as coal burners (which is why they did not use the cab-forward orientation), and initially SP assigned them to its Tucumcari Line in New Mexico. In later years, the locomotives were converted to oil operation, and most finished their careers on SP's desolate Modoc Line, a freight route connecting Fernley, Nevada, with Klamath Falls, Oregon, by way of Alturas, California.

During World War II, Minnesota iron hauler Duluth, Missabe & Iron Range was in great need of

Norfolk & Western operated one of the last large North American steam fleets, using them to haul coal, merchandise freight, and passengers through the 1950s. An N&W eastbound coal train is seen near Montvale, Virginia, on April 17, 1958. *George Diamond*

motive power to move iron ore from mines in the Range to its docks on Lake Superior at Duluth and Superior. Ore was then shipped by way of the Great Lakes to steel-producing centers in Indiana, Ohio, and Pennsylvania. The war resulted in a record need for steel, and the DM&IR had never been busier. In 1943, with authority from the War Production Board, Baldwin built 19 Yellowstones for Iron Range service. They were very similar to NP's originals constructed 15 years earlier, but since they were not required to burn low-grade fuel, they had smaller fireboxes and 125-square-foot grates. These were small compared to NP's, which as it turned out did not require their huge fireboxes and DM&IR's fireboxes were eventually shortened to slightly more reasonable dimensions. The very last Yellowstones were also war babies built by Baldwin: a fleet of beautifully proportioned locomotives designed for heavy service on the Baltimore & Ohio, class EM-1.

Cab-Forward

Southern Pacific was faced with an unusual operating problem in its strategic Donner Pass crossing. Part of the original 1869 Transcontinental Railroad, and a main artery to the West, much of the line was covered by long snowsheds, operated through numerous tunnels, and featured one of the longest sustained grades in North America. This combination had made running conventionally oriented Mallet Compounds difficult because smoke and noxious gases tended to fill the cab, asphyxiating the crew. In order to overcome this difficulty and take advantage of the superior pulling power of the Mallet Compound, which SP desperately needed on this heavily traveled route, SP decided to turn the Mallet around and run it "cab forward." This arrangement was possible because SP's

Norfolk & Western perfected the Mallet compound years after most North American railways had abandoned the type in favor of simple articulated locomotives. N&W 2156, one of 16 Y6a's built in 1942, is seen working as a pusher between Roanoke and Bluefield, Virginia, in 1958. *Donald Fellows*

engines burned oil instead of coal, so the fuel could easily be pumped from the tender to the firebox. SP's unorthodox approach was viewed with skepticism when it was introduced, but proved extremely effective, and soon SP was operating an entire fleet of cab-forward Mallet Compounds.

In the late 1920s, when Mallets were falling out of favor, Southern Pacific contemplated retiring the cab-forward concept but instead chose to rebuild its unique cab-forward articulateds as simple engines. The rebuilt articulateds were very successful. They were capable of faster mountain running and produced 10 percent more tractive effort than compounds. Southern Pacific was so pleased with the performance of its simple articulated locomotives, it decided to purchase a fleet of new locomotives based on their design. In 1929, Baldwin delivered the first new simple articulateds, which further improved on the performance of the older rebuilt engines. The new locomotives, class AC-4 4-8-8-2s, featured 63-inch drivers, used slightly larger fireboxes and cylinders, operated at a higher boiler pressure (235 psi versus 210 psi) than the converted Mallets, and delivered 112,760 pounds tractive effort—significantly more power than the older engines. During the next 15 years, Baldwin built eight classes of 4-8-8-2 cab-forwards for SP, totaling 195 locomotives. Classes AC-4 through AC-6 were very similar to one another, and the later semistreamlined locomotives were classes AC-7, AC-8, AC-10, AC-11, and AC-12.

Challengers

Articulated types had traditionally been limited to relatively slow speed operation. While simple articulated engines could run significantly faster

On July 31, 1958, a Norfolk & Western A Class 1233 leads an eastbound mixed freight at Blue Ridge, Virginia. One of N&W's big Y class 2-8-8-2 Mallet Compounds is shoving hard on the rear of the train. N&W developed the A class simple articulated in 1936 for high-speed mainline service, and ultimately N&W built 43 of the type. *Richard Jay Solomon*

than older Mallet Compounds, they were not expected to run faster than about 40 miles per hour because of front-end stability problems.

In 1936, Union Pacific introduced the 4-6-6-4 type, which featured 69-inch drivers and delivered 97,400 pounds tractive effort. The combination of four-wheel leading truck for better front-end stability, a high-capacity firebox and boiler, tall drivers, and the flexibility afforded by an articulated wheelbase produced a powerful, adaptable locomotive capable of running at 60 to 70 miles per hour. The 4-6-6-4 could operate on most Union Pacific mainlines and was well suited for freight and passenger work. UP named the wheel arrangement the Challenger and

In 1941, Union Pacific expanded its successful 4-6-6-4 Challenger design into a 4-8-8-4, a truly enormous locomotive known as a Big Boy. In September 1956, Union Pacific Big Boy 4002 leads a refrigerated boxcar train over Sherman Hill at Perkins, Wyoming. Alco built a total of 25 Big Boys for Union Pacific; eight of them have been preserved. *Union Pacific Museum collection, image number 74488*

ultimately owned 105 of them. Challengers were regularly powered on UP's grade-intensive Los Angeles & Salt Lake route and were often used on lines west of North Platte, Nebraska, but were rarely assigned to flat areas further east.

The Challenger type enjoyed considerable popularity, and roughly 215 were built. In the West, Rio Grande, Northern Pacific, and Western Pacific used them, and eastern coal carriers Delaware & Hudson, Western Maryland, and Clinchfield all operated Challenger fleets with considerable success.

Norfolk & Western Articulateds

Norfolk & Western's highly individualistic policy toward locomotive development and application resulted in two very distinctive articulated designs; its Y class 2-8-8-2 Mallets and A class 2-6-6-4 simple articulateds. As mentioned earlier, N&W stayed with big steam longer than any other American carrier, so when all other lines had abandoned regular steam operations, N&W was still using its huge articulateds to haul coal.

N&W continued to build and refine the Mallet Compound more than two decades after most other lines had abandoned the type in favor of simple operation. The basis for its highly successful Mallet was the United States Railroad Administration 2-8-8-2 design that dated from World War I. (The USRA developed a host of successful, well-proportioned, standardized designs during the war when it controlled the American Railway network.) N&W continued to improve the design, and in 1936 it introduced its Y6, considered the ultimate Mallet type. It featured all the attributes of modern steam locomotive design, including a high-capacity boiler, cast-steel bed frames, mechanical lubrication systems, precision counterbalancing, and roller bearings. They were extraordinarily reliable locomotives; in 1953 they worked an average of 6,000 miles a month in heavy freight service. They could produce 132,000 pounds starting tractive effort as a compound locomotive. However, a special valve controlled by the engineer permitted operation at slow speeds as a simple locomotive, and in this capacity, the engine could deliver an astounding 170,000 pounds tractive effort. While the Y6s usually operated at just 20 to 30 miles per hour, they were not the ponderous slow machines typecast by early Mallet Compounds, but were capable of 50 miles per hour in regular service.

Although it remained committed to the Mallet, in the 1930s Norfolk & Western also developed the simple articulated for high-speed service; its 2-6-6-4 class A was among the railroad's achievements. It featured 70-inch drivers, 24x30-inch cylinders, and its boiler operated at 300 psi to produce 114,000 pounds starting tractive effort. When running at 35 to 40 miles per hour, the A would develop roughly 5,500 horsepower. It could easily maintain 70 miles per hour with a heavy passenger train or haul a 15,500-ton freight 112 miles in four hours.

The Largest Steam

In 1939, Electro-Motive debuted the freight diesel, a four-unit streamlined locomotive, known as the FT. This machine and its successors would ultimately purge steam from American rails—save for excursions and publicity runs. However, this new technology didn't kill steam right away, nor did it discourage the steam builders from constructing some of the largest and most powerful locomotives ever built.

Between 1941 and 1944, Alco built 25 4-8-8-4s for Union Pacific. This enormous, magnificent machine is known as the "Big Boy," a locomotive frequently miscredited as the largest steam locomotive ever built. For a short time, it was the largest and the heaviest at 772,000 pounds, but Chesapeake & Ohio's 2-6-6-6 Allegheny, first built in 1942, is slightly heavier than the Big Boy. Lima built 60 Alleghenies for C&O and another 8 for Virginian. While the C&O Allegheny is often listed as

After diesels took over on Southern Pacific's mountain grades, SP transferred some of its cab-forward simple articulateds to the Bay Area where they worked until the mid-1950s. On September 8, 1956, SP AC-11 4267 leads an eastbound freight past the sugar refinery at Crocket, California. *Fred Matthews*

Disney's Touchstone Productions borrowed Southern Pacific GS-4 4449 to film the movie, *Tough Guys*, in 1986. Here, the "Disney Daylight" steams south toward Los Angeles through Chittenden Pass on SP's fabled Coast Route on March 8, 1986, on the way to a starring role in an otherwise silly movie. *Brian Jennison*

weighing slightly less than the Big Boy, it is actually the heaviest at 775,330 pounds.

UP's Big Boy was an expansion of its successful Challenger design. It used 68-inch drivers, four 23.75x32-inch cylinders, operated at 300 psi, and produced 135,375 pounds tractive effort—approximately 40 percent more than UP's Challengers. At 40 miles per hour, the Big Boy was capable of delivering between 7,000 and 7,500 horsepower, considerably more than even the most modern, powerful diesel electrics built today. Unlike the Challenger, which was designed to operate all over Union Pacific, the Big Boy was intended to operate on the railroad's mainline across Wyoming between Cheyenne, Wyoming, and Ogden, Utah. Although often assigned to graded territory, the Big Boy was not a slow machine. It could easily maintain 60 miles per hour.

C&O's Alleghenies were assigned to the Allegheny subdivision, between Hinton, West Virginia, and Clifton, Virginia, and worked primarily in heavy coal service. They were the most powerful locomotives ever built with six sets of drivers, and they could deliver 110,000 pounds tractive effort, significantly more than UP's Challengers.

A pair of C&O Alleghenies could routinely pull loaded coal trains weighing in excess of 11,000 tons up the 0.6 percent grade over Allegheny summit. This was not an exceptionally steep grade, however, it represented a tremendous operating challenge, and the Lima-built Allegheny's solo performances moving such heavy trains are still considered some of the greatest achievements of the steam era. Many authorities have deemed the Allegheny as Lima's finest locomotive.

GLOSSARY

American Standard or American Type: A steam locomotive with a 4-4-0 wheel arrangement. It was the most popular variety of locomotive in the nineteenth century.

Atlantic type: A steam locomotive with a 4-4-2 wheel arrangement.

Berkshire type: A steam locomotive with a 2-8-4 wheel arrangement, named for the Berkshire Hills in western Massachusetts.

boiler pressure: The operating pressure in locomotive boiler, typically between 150 and 300 psi.

booster: An auxiliary steam engine on a locomotive used at slow speeds for starting heavy trains. The booster typically engages the rear trailing truck or a tender truck.

compound locomotive: A locomotive with two sets of cylinders, which improves the thermal efficiency by double expansion of the steam.

cylinder cutoff: Limiting steam intake into the cylinders, which allows for greater steam expansion and results in more efficient steam usage and lower fuel consumption.

double heading: The operation of two locomotives, each with its own crew. This was necessary when more power was required to move a train than a single locomotive could provide.

drivers: A steam locomotive's driving wheels, the wheels that power the locomotive. A locomotive with a 4-8-4 wheel arrangement has eight driving wheels.

duplex: A nonarticulated locomotive with two complete sets of running gear.

dynamic augment: Destructive pounding forces caused by an imbalance of driving wheels and reciprocating parts.

eight-coupled type: Any locomotive with eight driving wheels coupled together.

feedwater heater: An energy-saving device that preheats water before introducing it to the boiler.

firebox: Where the fire is made to heat the boiler water.

firebox grate: Where the fire sits in the firebox. One of several important measures of a locomotive's potential.

high-drivers: Tall driving wheels; on modern locomotives usually those with a radius of 70 inches or more.

Hudson-type: A steam locomotive with a 4-6-4 wheel arrangement.

less-than-carload traffic: Small shipments that occupy less than one boxcar, typically high-value goods that require expedited schedules and special treatment.

main rods: The rods on the side of a locomotive that transmit power from the cylinders to the main driving wheel and siderods. The siderods transmit power to the remaining driving wheels.

Mallet compound: An articulated compound locomotive where the front portion of the engine is hinged to the rear frame but not rigidly attached to the boiler, allowing the engine needed flexibility in tight curves.

Mikado type: A steam locomotive with a 2-8-2 wheel arrangement.

Mohawk: New York Central's name for its 4-8-2 locomotives.

Mountain type: A steam locomotive with a 4-8-2 wheel arrangement.

Niagara: New York Central's name for its 4-8-4 locomotives.

Northern type: A steam locomotive with a 4-8-4 wheel arrangement. One of just several names for this arrangement.

psi: Abbreviation for pounds per square inch.

simple engine: A locomotive that uses multiple sets of cylinders that are all at the same pressure, instead of compounded. (*See* compound locomotive.)

superheated steam: A steam superheater recirculates boiler steam through tubes in enlarged boiler flues, raising steam temperature by at least 200°F before it enters the cylinders. Superheated steam stores more heat energy in a given volume of steam, thereby increasing its expansive power in the cylinders.

ten-coupled type: Any locomotive with 10 driving wheels coupled together.

Texas type: A steam locomotive with a 2-10-4 wheel arrangement.

tractive effort: The tractive force of a locomotive, a figure that is used to compare the potential output of a locomotive.

valve gear: Equipment serving a function similar to the transmission in an automobile. Typically a combination of rods and eccentric cranks that regulate the passage of steam to the cylinders in order to maximize the efficiency of the engine and control the direction of its output.

STEAM LOCOMOTIVE FACT BARS

Boston & Albany A-1

    Wheel arrangement: 2-8-4, Berkshire

    Cylinders (bore x stroke): 28x30 inches

    Driving wheels: 63 inches

    Firebox grate: 100 square feet

    Engine weight: 389,000 pounds

    Tractive effort: 81,400 pounds

Nickel Plate Road S-3

    Wheel arrangement: 2-8-4, Berkshire

    Cylinders: 25x34 inches

    Driving wheels: 69 inches

    Firebox grate: 90.3 square feet

    Engine weight: 444,290 pounds

    Tractive effort: 64,100 pounds

Texas & Pacific I-1

    Wheel arrangement: 2-10-4, Texas

    Cylinders: 29x32 inches

    Driving wheels: 63 inches

    Firebox grate: 100 square feet

    Engine weight: 448,000 pounds

    Tractive effort: 83,000 pounds (plus 13,000 pounds with booster)

New York Central J-1a

    Wheel arrangement: 4-6-4, Hudson

    Cylinders: 25x28 inches

    Driving wheels: 79 inches

    Firebox grate: 81.5 square feet

    Engine weight: 343,000 pounds

    Tractive effort: 42,300 pounds

New York Central J-3a

    Wheel arrangement: 4-6-4, Hudson

    Cylinders: 22.5x29 inches

    Driving wheels: 79 inches

    Firebox grate: 82 square feet

    Engine weight: 360,000 pounds

    Tractive effort: 43,440 pounds

Milwaukee Road F-7

    Wheel arrangement: 4-6-4

    Cylinders: 23.5x30 inches

    Driving wheels: 84 inches

    Firebox grate: 96.5 square feet

    Engine weight: 415,000 pounds

    Tractive effort: 50,300 pounds

Canadian Pacific H1e

    Wheel arrangement: 4-6-4, Royal Hudson

    Cylinders: 22x30 inches

    Driving wheels: 75 inches

    Firebox grate: 80.8 square feet

    Engine weight: 365,400 pounds

    Tractive effort: 45,300 pounds (plus 12,000 pounds with booster)

New York Central S-1a

    Wheel arrangement: 4-8-4, Niagara

    Cylinders: 25x32 inches

    Driving wheels: 75 inches

    Firebox grate: 100.1 square feet

    Engine weight: 471,000 pounds

    Tractive effort: 62,500 pounds

Norfolk & Western J Class

Wheel arrangement: 4-8-4

Cylinders: 27x32 inches

Driving wheels: 70 inches

Firebox grate: 107.7 square feet

Engine weight: 494,000 pounds

Tractive effort: 73,000 pounds

Southern Pacific GS-4

Wheel arrangement: 4-8-4, Northern

Cylinders: 25.5x32 inches

Driving wheels: 80 inches

Firebox grate: 90.4 square feet

Engine weight: 475,000 pounds

Tractive effort: 64,760 pounds (plus 13,000 pounds with booster)

Santa Fe 2900 class

Wheel arrangement: 4-8-4, Northern

Cylinders: 28x32 inches

Driving wheels: 80 inches

Firebox grate: 108 square feet

Engine weight: 510,150 pounds

Tractive effort: 66,000 pounds

Reading T-1

Wheel arrangement: 4-8-4, Northern

Cylinders: 27x32 inches

Driving wheels: 70 inches

Firebox grate: 94.5 square feet

Engine weight: 441,300 pounds

Tractive effort: 68,000 pounds (plus 11,100 pounds with booster)

Chesapeake & Ohio J-3-A

Wheel arrangement: 4-8-4, Greenbrier

Cylinders: 27.5x30 inches

Driving wheels: 72 inches

Firebox grate: 100.3 square feet

Engine weight: 479,400 pounds

Tractive effort: 68,300 pounds (plus 12,400 pounds with booster)

Norfolk & Western A Class

Wheel arrangement: 2-6-6-4

Cylinders: 24x30 inches (4 total)

Driving wheels: 70 inches

Firebox grate: 122 square feet

Engine weight: 573,000 pounds

Tractive effort: 114,000 pounds

Union Pacific Challenger

Wheel arrangement: 4-6-6-4, Challenger

Cylinders: 21x32 inches (4 total)

Driving wheels: 69 inches

Firebox grate: 132.2 square feet

Engine weight: 627,000 pounds

Tractive effort: 97,350 pounds

Union Pacific Big Boy

Wheel arrangement: 4-8-8-4, Big Boy

Cylinders: 23.75x32 inches (4 total)

Driving wheels: 68 inches

Firebox grate: 150.3 square feet

Engine weight: 772,000 pounds

Tractive effort: 135,375

Northern Pacific Z-5

Wheel arrangement: 2-8-8-4, Yellowstone

Cylinders: 26x32 inches (4 total)

Driving wheels: 63 inches

Firebox grate: 182 square feet

Engine weight: 717,000 pounds

Tractive effort: 140,000 pounds (plus 13,400 pounds with booster)

INDEX